The Making of a Successful Business Woman

Compiled by Telishia Berry

Publisher of *Courageous Woman Magazine*

ISBN-13: 978-0-9786001-4-3

Strive Publishing is a division of Courageous Media Group. For more information on the authors, ordering, book signings, or to sponsor an event, contact us at: info@courageouswomanmag.com

Edited/formatted by Shonell Bacon

Cover designed by Tanya Roquemore and Oladimeji Basit Alaka

Contents

Acknowledgments

Thank you for my four reflections that inspire me to keep going: Kendre', Tisha, Toi, and Kennedy.

I also acknowledge and give thanks to editor Shon Bacon for her expertise and work on our books to Editorial Manager Dr. Ladel Lewis for her tireless contributions.

Introduction

According to information presented by the National Association of Women Business Owners, more than 11.6 million firms are owned by women, employing nearly 9 million people and generating $1.7 trillion in sales as of 2017.

Women are slightly more likely to start a business than men, as the Score report states, and an article on smallbiztrends.com showed that 62% of women entrepreneurs depend on their business as their primary source of income.

Entrepreneurship may not be for everyone. But for those who decide to give it a try, here is a sobering statistic. According to the data from the Bureau of Labor of Statistics, about 50% of small businesses fail by their fifth year. Some reasons may include wars, recessions, high taxation, poor management, lack of marketing, and inability to compete with other similar businesses or simply the public's lack of interest in their products or services.

That doom and gloom statistic hasn't put a damper on the start-up plans of today's courageous women. Today, women-owned businesses are increasing five times faster than the national average, and four out of ten businesses are owned by women.

Are you a woman who has put some thought into starting your own business? Is being your own boss or CEO a dream you want to fulfill?

The Making of a Successful Business Woman provides key tactics on how to survive in business. There are chapters that deal with all elements of business development and growth. There is a chapter that explains how to successfully network with future clients and collaborators. Other chapters emphasize pressing through the tough times, staying focused and committed to the process, and in closing, there is a guide full of helpful business start-up info.

If you are ready to be courageous and join the ranks of the many women in business, this book shares stories of 20 empowered entrepreneurs.

The Making of a Successful Business Woman serves as an inspirational resource to guide you along your entrepreneurial journey with great details and true-to-life stories by women who have accomplished their goals and dreams of successfully running their own business. I hope this book will be the motivation you need to launch your business!

Telishia Berry

With God, Motivation, and Determination, There Are No Limits

Jeanette Abney

My name is Jeanette Abney. I am currently a licensed marriage family therapist, owner of two out- patient counseling centers (The Center For The Treatment Of Addiction Inc. and JA Precious Inc.) with multiple locations. I also host a weekly podcast at Blog Talk Radio titled *Precious Predicaments*. One would say that I must be of Jamaican descent as a comedian once put it. However, I am a woman with a purpose. Having multiple business has been an interesting journey. However, the rewards of assisting others is priceless.

It has been said that God has a sense of humor. I am honored and enjoy the services I provide, yet I often failed to understand God's humor. Nor did I find owning a business financially lucrative. The service I provide is priceless. Over the years, my adult daughter also frequently reminds me of my quote, "Next year is going to be better." And I must say many years have come and gone. I am proud to say the employees at my local bank treat me like I am a star even when my account is overdrawn.

I was raised by a single mother in the city of Compton. My mother Rejean Brooks made sure that her three daughters would make it in life. She had a unique parenting style. I also believe that some of her parenting techniques should have had her placed under the jail house. Her actions caused many emotional scars to me and my sisters. However, those scars propelled me to birth *Precious Predicaments* on Voice America and then on Blog Talk Radio. This was my way of keeping her memory alive as she succumbed to breast cancer in 2008.

My mother always told me that with an education I can do whatever I wanted to do as far as a career. I later learned that such was not true. I was often ahead of others in my class and frequently bored as I thought I was smarter than most of my teachers… and my mother. As my life continued, I later continued to pursue my education despite facing other life challenges and failed relationships. I later learned that I was considered a threat to many individuals because I am an outspoken, educated, articulated African-American woman. Such thoughts from others played a role in my life that followed me for years. They also helped me as I became a business woman.

As a child, I often spoke of becoming an attorney and retiring as a judge. I never liked politics and often was punished by my mother for some of the comments that I made as a child as they related to political matters. To avoid getting in trouble and knowing that I could not keep my mouth closed, I knew this was not going to be the occupation for me. So like many, I had a few options. In fact, I had two: one was an occupation that I saw many family members work in—a school bus driver, and the other was to work at a bakery like my mother, who was employed for thirty-three years at Dolly Madison prior to her retirement. Working at a bakery was not going to be in my best interest because I had a special relationship with food. I would have made Jenny Craig have an emotional breakdown because I had a lifetime membership at a 24-hour fitness center, and they saw me like individuals that only go to church on the holidays. Therefore, at the age of eighteen, obtaining my license to drive a school bus sounded pretty good. So, I became a bus driver while living in Compton.

In 1986, I married and moved to Oceanside, California, and as you can imagine with me being strong willed and articulate, I frequently got in trouble. I received several threats of being terminated from my jobs. I have had to file complaints and lawsuits. At 33, I retired due to injuries sustained; it was a scary time, yet I felt I did not have a choice as my knee let me know that it was time to give it up—not to mention getting up early in the morning was not for me.

Retiring from my job was a life-changing moment for me; however, I had to put on my big girl underwear and, like my daughter used to tell me, "figure it out."

As a mother of two and having married and divorced a few times, I continued pursuing my education. It seemed like no matter what degree I obtained, employers told me I needed a higher degree. Throughout my life, I endured several life challenges. I endured failures as they related to many aspects of my life, yet I never viewed myself as a failure. That does not mean that I did not accept responsibility for my role. I just knew that there were some things that I wanted out of life, and I was determined to get them. What I had to do was learn how to fight differently. I had to learn that many of my friends were not my friends. There were going to be times that I would have to stand alone, not be understood or supported even by those that said they loved me. I also had to learn that rejection was not always a bad thing. I recalled a lawyer once telling me, as he was representing me against the school district, that I did not fit in. Sentiments such as this became more of a norm, which I later learned to embrace. It also built muscles that the gym could not give me. I knew then I could not work for others.

As I continued to find my way, I later became a social worker. I wanted to make a difference in the lives of abused children. It was then that I had a supervisor share with me, "With God, motivation, and determination, you can do whatever you want." I never forgot those words. I tried to always keep things in that order—God, motivation, and determination—no matter what life threw my way. I also recall stating to another, "If you are not going to be part of the solution, don't add to the problem." I had to teach individuals how to treat me by respecting others as I am to be respected. Just because one is a business owner does not mean that one will receive the respect of others.

With that being said, I am proud of the woman that I am today. I purchased a business in 2006 after meeting the prior owner in 2005. I believe what he may have meant for evil God turned it into something good. I did not know an LLC from an S or a C Corp. I had no business knowledge and, till this day, still get upset when my daughter asks me about a budget. However, if God brings one to something, he will make sure that they are equipped to get his job done. I did not purchase a business because I had money, a business plan, or investors. I stepped out on faith and did my part to please God and made it work. I made several sacrifices and perhaps a few mistakes. Yet, I truly enjoy working to strengthen families and advocate for those who are afraid to fight for themselves. I educate individuals from all walks of life as I teach them to respect and communicate effectively with others as they may disagree yet do not have to disrespect.

I have learned that wisdom far exceeds knowledge. Be patient and use wisdom. Never be afraid to step out on faith, yet trust and listen to God and not you because when God is in it, things will work out. Discouragement will come. Negativity will sound normal. However, if one surrounds themselves with positive and wise individuals, they will help guide you in the right direction. And yes, professional jealousy is real, and everybody will not like you. And that is ok as long as you will be willing to stand alone and love yourself. God will guide you. Motivation will keep you going. And determination will remind you to never give up. And when it is time to retire, relax and enjoy the fruit of your labor.

Jeanette Abney provides services that delivers real help as she motivates others to change as well as restore relationships.

Get Ready for the Valley and the Mountain

Dr. Yashima AziLove

I was ready.

In the words of Lorraine Hansberry, I was "Young, Gifted and Black." A Pentecostal bishop's daughter with an Ivy League degree. I managed multimillion-dollar budgets and made a multi-six-digit salary with bonuses, options, and perks. I purchased my first home at 25 as a single woman and, with time, had a growing modest real estate portfolio. I was newly married by choice, not thirst and was a new mother of a sickly premature baby boy who changed everything.

I knew God and business. I had a network and a skill set. I had a bank account and vision. I had drive and supporters.

I was so ready.

I also had years of managers "coaching" me on my 'It Factor.' They'd tell me, "Yashima, you're a star. You have a commanding presence and a tremendous skill set, but you should tone it down some." Blank faced for over 10 years, I'd ask, "What is my 'It Factor' and if it's a good thing, why should I tone it down?"

I was full of personal insecurities and often struggled with seasons of depression compounded by years of low self-esteem. I didn't wear it. I was a preacher's daughter. I was groomed to mask my emotions and scars for the benefit of serving others. I thought that was normal. So, I did it every day of my business life. Year after year. Company after company. Manager after manager.

I was promoted for my ability, but something about this 'It Factor' that made me oh so good, also bought me so much pain. I was an articulate, well-groomed black girl who represented the company well...until I upstaged a white counterpart. I was the cool black girl in the corner office until I wasn't black enough for some. In time, my inability to identify and control this 'IT' strangled me.

Apparently, I was a convenient 'IT' for white folks and too much 'IT' for black folks.

I lived a dichotomy. They promoted me but wanted to kill my shine. They cheered for me, but they hated me. I was successful, but I lived empty.

Until my son.

"We have to take him...NOW!"

The last words I could hear before I delivered a two-pound three-ounce baby boy amidst the crisis of my very broken marriage; the chaos of my career; the pain of my depression; and the trauma of God allowing this all to happen to me.

So, I quit.

I quit my job. I quit the people whose voices generated the most noise and confusion for me. I quit the lifestyle that didn't know if it wanted to embrace or reject me.

I could no longer live numb. I was someone's mother.

I started a business.

At the wise counsel of a lifelong friend, I needed a powerful business name. It needed to be meaningful and not merely commercial, but something that fueled me. The moment Sean Cunningham said it, I knew – MAGNATE. It means – stand out in a crowd; dominate; master; a mogul.

June 10, 2014, the day I owned my 'IT.'

Magnate was born. And then it was just me with a phone, a computer, and my 'IT.'

Oh, and a sickly son. And a loving husband who fought alongside of me to heal our marriage after years of separation, who was laid off his job less than 30 days after I quit. Like, really?!

In days, my 'IT' couldn't withstand the instant lack of financial stability, medical insurance, private school tuition, mortgages, and car notes built on a multi six-digit salary that became a $0 income household overnight.

I stopped.

Yes, I knew God, but I stopped. The silence of the office phone. The emptiness of my inbox. The growing amnesia of my network. The deletion of my name from guest lists.

I broke.

The mounting white envelopes on my kitchen counter.

I sunk…but God!

Love lifted me, and faith carried me from turbulence to triumphant.

I shared excerpts of my deeply personal story in the middle of this business building book for one reason. I want you to PAUSE and survey your life. The business you're embarking upon is not just a money generating activity. Entrepreneurship must be purpose driven.

Many people elevate business ownership as the ultimate position of power and freedom in contrast to a corporate career. I disagree. Your purpose must be fulfilled despite your career track. Seek your purpose first, and then assess which path actually leads you to it. This is a highly introspective journey.

There are corporate executives paid salaries that far exceed the average small business income. Your decision can't be financial.

Most corporate executives have four to six weeks paid vacation. Business owners never "get paid" to vacate and for many, the struggle of finding disposable income to travel is real. Your decision can't be about perceived "freedom" when you aren't free to take a vacation or have a sick day when you want or need to.

Corporate executives have a staff to execute their vision. This is rarely the case for entrepreneurial service providers. There is no team on day one, or day 365 for that matter. You must be prepared to be a visionary, strategist, and grunt worker. Your decision can't be ego driven and title based.

You get the point.

I lived bi-vocationally for many years until living both no longer felt congruent. Today, I run a global professional development firm full time because it is my destiny place for this season of my life. Here's the secret – I'd go back to big business tomorrow if I genuinely believed it was my next destiny step. My point - know your purpose AND your season. Your career trajectory is as deeply personal as your decision for a spouse. You have to live with it!

That said, there are lessons you can glean from others so you are informed and equipped for your journey. As my grandma Margaret would say, "Eat the meat and throw away the bone." I hope as you explore my chapter and the others of this book, you will eat the wisdom and discard only the bone.

Here are a few business snackables.

1. **Count the cost. See the risks.** Business ownership may be what you aspire to do, but never pursue it in isolation. It must make sense

for your life. Would I have knowingly went into ownership with a husband who wasn't working, no healthcare benefits and a lifestyle built to be sustained on salaries that were no longer existent? No.

The hustle ownership forced me into at that season of my life complicated an already difficult journey. Better timing and good planning would have given me the luxury of learning and failing time. Your business impacts your family and life. It may not be a family business, but it is a family affair. I've coached more business owners than I care to admit who paid the price of entrepreneurship with their marriage and health. Count the cost.

Do a life check. Is now the right time? Is your spouse supportive? Are your children independent? Do you have six months of life expenses saved with an additional three-month emergency fund?

2. **Have a clear, unwavering, and authentic WHY.** My pride reminded me how much money my work generated for 'the man.' My heart was driven by more time with my son. My thirst was driven by financial possibilities. My mind needed a new challenge. My spirit craved for purpose. I'm telling you, my WHYs were all over the place! The confusion did not serve me well. There must be a compelling reason to take this leap of faith and continue in it that transcends the moments of intense darkness that will inevitably come.

Do a WHY check. Why are you doing this? What do you expect to achieve through business ownership that you can't doing something else? Are you running from something, or running toward your purpose?

3. **Don't be shy**. If you're good – you better be okay telling someone. There is no room for 'shy' in business.

I'm a severe Myers Briggs introvert. No one, with the exception of my husband, believes this. From singing solos in church at the age of three, to my career in journalism, marketing, and ministry - I live a very public life. Painfully so. It's a learned behavior - a switch. I power on, as needed and when I shut down… only my husband sees the crash. He protects me from the burn.

In business, you are the chief marketing officer, and you are the sales executive. Clients won't 'know' until you tell them. You can't be modest in your presentation. If you can solve the problem – say so. Hiding any part of your 'It' due to your discomfort is as much out of integrity as promising outcomes you know you can't deliver.

I should add—rejection comes with the territory. They are denying your service or product, not you. Know the difference.

Do a temperament check. Are you comfortable writing and talking about yourself or product? How do you manage rejection and stress? Are you comfortable marketing and selling?

4. **Your expert skill doesn't qualify you for ownership.** When you are in the corporate world, CEO means Chief Executive Officer. However, in the entrepreneurial world, CEO means Chief EVERYTHING Officer. On day one, you don't have the luxury of being an expert solely. I was a great communicator and marketer, but I hated accounting, sales and checking voicemail. My list of what drained the entrepreneurial life out of me was longer than that which fueled me.

I was expected to do it all, until I realized I couldn't afford NOT to hire people to focus on my weaknesses. I needed to spend more time doing what I loved. When you aren't making any money – roll up your sleeves and expect to do everything. When there's a little money – make a decision. You must decide if you're going to work in or on your business.

With a limited income, I took a leap of faith and hired my first virtual assistant. I contracted a W9 team to manage through the work that drained my energy. Something magical happened. I found my sweet spot, and it wasn't what I expected.

Do a skill check. What management necessities, other than your expertise, can you competently do to keep your business afloat? Do you have access to experts to do what you can't do?

5. **Go with the flow and listen to the whispers.** Where you start is seldom where you finish. Once I received the help needed in my business and I tapped into a flow, I realized the greatest

> value I brought to my clients was not in my marketing work, but in the consulting and coaching I naturally provided. Everything in my background until that moment of clarity pointed to me remaining in the marketing communications discipline.

I listened to the whispers.

My clients were telling me how easy I was to speak with and how much clarity they gained from our exchanges. I was increasingly asked to conduct team building meetings. My spirit was no longer fulfilled solely in marketing communications. I longed for more.

I followed the flow.

Clarity was birthed. Communications was still at the core of my work, but my fulfillment was now found in professional development – training, coaching and consulting corporations, celebrities and cultural influencers.

Don't be afraid to shift. Revising your business plan and changing direction is not failure and defeat, but the evidence of clarity and purpose. And where there is purpose, prosperity follows.

I am ready.

Today, I'm called from around the globe to speak with audiences seeking to be empowered and tooled for leadership, self-mastery and marketplace success.

I'm contracted at some of the top global companies in the world. My 'It' is expected, celebrated and compensated.

I am so ready.

Marriage, restored. My son, healed. Purpose, manifesting. Divine favor overtakes me. Comfortable in my skin. My phone is ringing, and my inbox is full. My cup runs over.

I am MAGNATE.

Get ready.

You're next.

Dr. Yashima AziLove is a multifaceted marketplace mogul and minister whose professional aptitude and spiritual depth has served corporate, celebrity, and faith audiences around the world. Dr. Yashima founded Magnate Consulting, a professional development firm providing consulting, coaching and training services in leadership development, self-mastery, and brand communications after over twenty years of executive level marketing communication roles in the insurance, financial services, healthcare, and entertainment industries. From the sacred to the secular, she is a sought-after speaker, media commentator and ICF certified professional coach with a global client footprint. Dr. Yashima is a graduate of the University of Pennsylvania, Annenberg School of Communications and Wharton School of Business;

she holds a Doctor of Divinity degree. She is the proud wife of N. Emmanuel AziLove and mother of son, Malachi.

Learn more about Dr. Yashima and her work on Instagram (handle: Dr.Yashima), Twitter, Facebook (handle DrYashima for both Tw and FB), and her website: www.MagnateConsult.com.

It All Matters, Doesn't It?

Business Insights from the Journey of a Christian Playwright and Indie Filmmaker

D. Tina Batten

Humble beginnings, difficult to shake off. Honestly, why would you? I recall my humble beginnings in life and in business. My family still can't believe how I'm able to ration food like I do. If ever a national disaster, I would be the one who had enough food to ration until help comes. I always have a protein bar, water, nuts, and other snack items close by my side. I recently had the family over, and we prepared dinner. Cooking in the kitchen together is always a delight. I had one sweet potato that I baked in the oven. My thoughts, I have it, why not use it as an extra side dish? I sliced that one sweet potato so the four of us could share. The room silenced as we served our plates. They all looked at me with this odd look on their faces, but said nothing.

I was instructed a long time ago whenever I had the opportunity to speak or minister in front of large audiences, don't be afraid of their faces. So, I didn't think anything of it at the time. That is until a week after dinner. My mom and sister joked and laughed so hard about how they were still hungry and could not believe how I rationed out that one sweet potato to share with four grown adults. Of course, other food items were prepared, such as chicken breast, rice, and vegetables. My guess, they really wanted more sweet potato. Can you imagine it, one sweet potato, thinly sliced long ways and shared in that manner?

In business, you will need to make rations. Supply rations, inventory rations, time rations, allowances, allocations, quotas, funds, and restrictions are needed from time to time to maintain a healthy, successful business. Knowing where you come from and where you're going in addition to lots of hard work provides an excellent road map to success. There's nothing wrong with recalling your humble beginnings from time to time. Learn from them and use those experiences to help grow your business. In doing so, it will help grow you as a person.

Start at your level. Who knows how long it would have taken me to raise enough start-up funds, purchase office space, and own all the necessary equipment needed to launch Sister Batten Productions. Starting at my level and using what I had at the time was the best thing for me. There were times when producing a stage play or dinner show that, simply stated, I needed props to design the space on a limited budget. I didn't let that stop me from doing the show the Lord placed on my heart. Instead, I went shopping right at home, borrowing props from my own house. My husband isn't a fan of that of course, but I had to make it work to the best of my ability. I'm still able to find props by searching local thrift shops, secondhand stores, and online. Props that could be used for multiple projects I found best to purchase and own myself. By doing so, I was able to rent larger items needed to finish designing the space. Work your budget. Thinking ahead by catching those great sales to help build that prop inventory is a definite way to be financially conscious. Making something out of nothing works even better if you're crafty.

Funny story, I needed a car for a scene I was shooting, and we own a Dodge Charger. The producer found police lights online, and when the footage was complete, the scene looked so authentic. It was fabulous! I had my husband view the finished trailer. He watched with this strange look on his face. He turned his head and said to me, "Is that my Charger?" I made light of the situation. But as the old saying goes, if only you could have been the fly on that wall to see his facial expression. It was hilarious! I couldn't help but laugh. The point is if I'd waited until the perfect time when I had everything together, my dream of entrepreneurship may have never come to pass.

If you're tech savvy, create an app. If baking or cooking is your thing, then start baking and cooking. Use your kitchen or rent a kitchen until you build up your business. Perhaps you are gifted in music: create workshops, teach from your home or online, and take advantage of those tax deductions. Same goes for whatever area of interest you are best gifted in. Use your talents. Be the best at your level. Start with what you have right now and work it! Learn and grow along the journey. Find creative ways to keep educating yourself. Attend business conferences, meetings, workshops. Join business groups that will help grow your knowledge in business. Keep developing your craft. The most important fact is that you started! Eventually, financial blessings will come your way. Continue to work hard building relationships, collaborations, and partnerships within your community, then reach out globally. The rest will come in due time. If you're a praying person, believing in faith, it will always come to fruition.

Not my only gig. Having multiple streams of revenue or residual income flowing through your business is very important for longevity. Do your research. Find different ways to increase your finances. As a writer, playwright, and filmmaker producing my own original works, there are many avenues I can actively pursue for streams of revenue, such as writer for hire, inspirational speaker, performing arts ministry, tours, film screenings, product sales, and more. Sky's the limit is my thought process. Be innovative! Be creative! Be Courageous! You Got This!

Quality over Quantity. We live in a "right now" society. Everything is fast-paced. The microwave is too slow. We have pressure cookers that crisp and brown meat in under thirty minutes. That's great news. We're very busy people. Time is of the essence. I understand goals, projections, and deadlines need to be fulfilled. I understand that you can't move so slow that you don't get anything accomplished either. I'm saying, don't sacrifice the quality of your business just to produce the numbers. There are times when I need to take six months or longer to work on a program. The outcome is that I'm able to promote that program for two years or longer, developing multiple streams of revenue from that one product. I used that time producing the best possible product to share with the world. The quality of that work leads to more work, other business leads, ventures, additional sales, and most importantly helps expand clientele, sponsorships, and partnerships. Your business is a direct representation of you. If you're going to do it, do it right the first time. Sometimes, you're only given one opportunity. Make it count.

Pay it forward. My first pastor was the person who gave me the chance to produce my very first stage play. He opened the doors of the church for me, and that partnership turned out to be a win-win situation. I was able to bless the church financially, which in turn, blessed me tremendously. I continue to pursue higher aspirations because of that opportunity to do something that had been laid heavy on my heart. To this day, I continue to seek out new talent, offering first-time experiences in theater, film, and performing arts ministry to those individuals ready, able, and talented, but didn't have a platform. Having the ability to bless others by paying it forward is a blessing to me. If you haven't done so, try it.

It ALL matters. Whether you are a newly formed startup or you've been in business for years, honesty and integrity matters. As stated earlier, your business is a direct representation of you. So, be the best possible version of yourself. If you own a customer-based business, treat those customers right. If you have employees, treat them in a manner you want to be treated. People matter. Be true to your word. Build a successful business using honesty and integrity. Work your business in excellence. Stay current by constantly growing in knowledge and understanding of your business industry. When building my business, I've learned there are times when I need to press through the mess to get blessed. I've learned to pray before making decisions or sudden movements that will affect my business.

To answer the question, "It all matters, doesn't it?" Yes! Remembering those humble beginnings and continuing to educate yourself in business matters. Starting at your level and working in excellence matters. Developing multiple streams of revenue or producing residual income matters. Quality over quantity and paying it forward all matters. Conducting your business with honesty and integrity definitely matters.

My prayer is that this chapter along with the reading of this entire book has encouraged you to step out and start your own business. Step out, courageous woman, and be the woman God created you to be. Work those gifts and talents. I leave you with one of my favorite scriptures, "For with God, nothing shall be impossible" (Luke 1:37).

Not only is **Sister Darlene "Tina" Batten** a loving mother, grandmother, and wife, she is also president and founder of Sister Batten Productions. She is a gifted visual storyteller who is passionate about bringing encouraging messages of inspiration and hope to every project she's involved with. Sister Batten has a unique way of developing and creating fascinating stories that touch the heart of everyone who views her work. Her stage plays, dinner shows, and films promise to take you on a journey of the highs and lows of everyday life demonstrated in the most entertaining way. Sister Batten's storytelling is portrayed in a realistic manner that touches on subject matters of today. She is an anointed woman of God who is on the battlefield for the Lord!

Originally born in Philadelphia, then later moved and grew up in the Bronx, New York, Sister Batten is an overcomer of obstacles and life issues such as broken home, violence and poverty, just to name a few. She is a dreamer who loves performing and creative arts. With the support of her family and community, she continues to step out on faith turning passion of filmmaking along with obedience to God from dream to reality. Not only has she been writing, directing, and producing original dramatic stage plays, dinner shows, concerts and special events for the past eighteen years and counting, she also continues to produce films that challenge the mindset of everyday thinking while overcoming micro budgets through God's FAVOR of INCREASE.

Sister Batten is honored, thrilled, and extremely excited to be included alongside with her fellow multi-talented authors in this *Courageous Woman* collaborative book project. She will continue to be an inspiration to all those around her, bringing forth hope, love, and joy to a dying world. With such a humble heart and desire to bring people together in unity, Sister Batten will continue her work as a visual storyteller, spreading the good news of Jesus Christ one project after the other.

Use What You Have

Telishia Berry

If you're a woman who has ever worn pantyhose all day, you can relate to that annoying feeling you get when you can't wait to get home to strip them off as soon as you get inside your house. You then work them down your legs and slam dunk them onto the floor as if you were an NBA player. Honestly, I have taken mine off in the car on the way home! But nevertheless, that's how I envision finally breaking free from working for someone else to working for myself.

I thought back as far as I could remember as to when my entrepreneurial spirit was first awakened. When I was little, I remember my mother reading lots of comic books. She had many of them around the house. I decided to find out what was on those pages that kept her so preoccupied. Needless to say, once I started to read the comic books, the funnies were not that entertaining to me. It was the ads that offered home-based business opportunities, including stuffing envelopes, selling Sea Monkeys, social security card plates, or magic cards that grabbed my attention. The thought of sitting at the dining room table stuffing envelopes seemed easy and grownup. But the thought of Sea Monkeys running around the house scared me. The fact that I was only about 10 years old and didn't have money to invest was also a major drawback, so I decided to continue to pursue my business ventures, but with more age appropriate, practical products, like selling Kool-Aid from a Kool-Aid stand (A TV Tray) The Kool-Aid popsicles made with ice trays from my grandparents' freezer were a hit and sold for five cents each. Now I was making some money, and that little business woman was brewing inside me, but since I don't think I had heard the word 'entrepreneurship' yet, I thought it was cute when I heard people say, "She's a little hustler, she's making that money."

The Money Excitement

My mother had also taught me how to braid hair on my baby doll. So cornrows became easy to do. By the time I was 13, I was braiding hair. My best client was my little cousin, Jeri. Her grandmother, my great-aunt Dora would send her over to get her hair shampooed and cornrowed every two weeks. It was a skill I acquired via my mom and one I enjoyed. That $10 per head was great, too.

As a teenager, I had some babysitting jobs, but for the most part, I enjoyed sales and sold things like Christmas cards and participated in school fundraisers, and those infamous Girl Scout Cookies. Yep, I was a proud Brownie and Girl Scout.

I dabbled in several Multi-Level Marketing projects that just didn't fly well for me. With Avon, I liked the products so much, but I spent all my profits on buying them. Most of the MLM businesses didn't give much commission, and although I didn't have to punch a clock and there was no dress code, it still felt like I was working a low-wage job for someone else. My cousin had a traveling boutique business, and I would assist her when she needed help doing home parties She took me to New York to the shopping district and other places where would buy products like costume jewelry, purses, and other accessories wholesale to resale at her parties. Years later, I began doing the boutique home-parties. It was fun and provided an income while raising my kids.

Mixing Marriage and Motherhood with Being an Entrepreneur

As life and time had its way, marriage and motherhood took precedence, but the entrepreneurial zeal persisted. I made use of that zeal in multiple ways. I wrote and produced several plays that were quite rewarding and financially successful, but stressful.

I created several home businesses including partnering with my then, ten-year-old son Kendre' to create birthday party invitations using his artwork.

After a while, it became apparent that working from home would be ideal for me with having small children. I continued to create home-based businesses using my acquired knowledge and skills. I did a bit of everything from hair braiding because I am also a licensed cosmetologist to child care because I was a mother of four and had taken classes in childcare, to marketing materials for beauty professionals because I had learned to use graphic design programs and I had knowledge of the beauty industry.

Learning Online Business

I was always on the internet for one reason or another. I was fascinated with the amount of information available for just about anything you wanted to know. I thought learning how to manage a business online would be a great advancement because I would be able to reach people outside of my family, friends, and community.

My ex-husband and I worked together often. In 2006, my then husband was a celebrity stylist who had lots of celebrity clients. Some of his clients included Wayne Brady, Judge Mathis, Darius McCrary, and many of the Los Angeles Lakers, including Lamar Odom and the late and great Kobe Bryant. I decided I wanted to help him leverage his business and extend it online, and I would operate the online division. I spent a lot of time researching and developing the business model. I didn't know how to build websites, so I found a service, "U Build It," that had the built-in software, and I created his first website. I included lots of info on barbering as well as pics of him with numerous celebrity clients. I even created an e-book, *How To Be A Celebrity Barber*. We created a haircutting instructional DVD and other downloadable products that drew followers from around the world. Before we knew it, there were 10,000 plus subscribers eager to know how to become a celebrity hair stylist.

Unfortunately, that marriage was wavering on shaky grounds and thus was the business, and as the relationship disintegrated, so did the multi-million-dollar business we were building. It was sad to see all the work go down the drain, but all was not lost. I learned so much about online business, and I applied that knowledge to my own project, Courageous Woman Blog, which was later changed to *Courageous Woman Magazine*.

Use What You Have

In 2012, relocating from Los Angeles back to my hometown of Flint, Michigan was a very hard decision to make. I had lived in California for twelve years. I didn't want to go back home, but I am so glad I did. I needed that time to regroup after leaving my marriage. *Courageous Woman Magazine* had been online for about three years when I got the desire to launch as a print publication. I was working as a mobile phlebotomist and was ready to do something more. I had a friend who owned a thriving publication in Detroit, and I asked him for advice. I asked him what I needed to do to take my magazine from online to print. He said I was gonna need at least $30,000 to start. I thought, wow, how am I going to do that. I looked in my bank account and I was missing some zeros. I only had $30 in my account. My son taught me how to use Adobe Photoshop, so I created my own brochure and carbon contract and used the $30 to buy copies. I then went out into the community talking about *Courageous Woman Magazine*. I got articles from family and friends and advertisers in the community, and with the first issue, we distributed 4,000 complimentary copies in the Flint community. *Courageous Woman Magazine* has readers worldwide. We are now publishing books and have featured over 140 women sharing their stories in our anthologies. And more to come

When people ask me for advice or tips on how to start a business, I ask them what they've done in their careers and what marketable skills they have. Most times, they don't even realize the amount of information or skills they have acquired working for someone else. I ask them what's the one thing they really enjoy doing and can that one thing be turned into a business or can they relay the work or service they provided on a job to a business for themselves. I think the best way to start a meaningful and fruitful business is to dig within yourself to create an outline of what you have from your personal skills to your job skills to your education. Doing that can help you get some direction and help you better visualize your full potential and all the possibilities. Then if you need to finance your business, do your research on funding sources, from banks to personal loans and crowd-funding. You may have to be your biggest supporter, investor, and believer. Don't be afraid to be creative, innovative, and outright bold and confident to make it happen. Where there is a will, there is always a way to start where you are and use what you have.

Telishia Berry is the publisher and CEO of the award-winning publication, *Courageous Woman Magazine*, author, speaker, playwright, and radio host. In addition to *The Making of a Successful Business Woman*, Telishia has published several anthologies that showcase over 130 authors, including the most recently published, Amazon #1 Best Seller *Girl, Get Up and Win*. She is the author of the novel, *The Baptist Junkie*, a best-selling Christian fiction drama about faith, family, and redemption. She also published the book, *What Is a Courageous Woman*, a collaborative book with 78 authors. Telishia has several more books to be released in 2020, including her personal story and a new anthology, *I Am My Sister's Keeper*. Telishia enjoys helping women get their books done.

Just Start

Wilma Blyden

Through my recently released book *She Designed the Life She Wanted – Four Women, Four Journeys, One Church*, I shared insight on how four women discovered comfort, clarity, and guidance in God's word despite the challenges they faced on their Christian journey.

When I was writing the book, I shared my journey of being restored with family, friends, and basically anyone who would listen. It was not long before people started contacting me asking questions about the process of restoration, and I started to share my knowledge. I have found that most people view restoration as going back to who they were before challenges or pain occurred in their lives. Through revelation, I understand restoration is reverting to who God has created you to be and not who you were before you experienced challenges or pain.

The book was written to inspire women and help them to be restored to who God created them to be. On the journey of helping women, I became a Christian author, inspirational speaker, coach, and the founder of a network, *She Designed the Life She Wanted.*

If I could choose one word to sum up the titles, it would be an Entrepreneur!

Coaching women within the network has its challenges. To overcome these challenges, women are not only provided with tools to succeed, but they are also coached to believe in themselves. Along the journey I've noticed that if the women are given strategies to help them believe, win and manifest, the strategies are of no benefit to them if they don't believe in themselves or believe they can succeed. I believe it's important to help others identify their purpose, not just by simply inspiring them, but working with them until they achieve their goals.

The network is aimed at women who are focused on self-improvement, growth, and are looking to design a meaningful, impactful, and joy-filled life. As an entrepreneur, in order to make an impact, I believe one must be able to effect change and implement results. I believe everyone is designed to reach a different set of people based on the experiences we have in our lives. If you are considering becoming an entrepreneur take a moment and ask yourself, *How am I effective? What problems do I solve and How am I the solution?*

The road to entrepreneurship is not straight; it's like a ride on a roller coaster. I've experienced good times, happy moments, growth, success, and encountered roadblocks in the form of unbelief, distractions, lack of finances, and self-doubt, among many others on this entrepreneurial journey. However, I don't allow the roadblocks to deter me from moving in the direction that I want my life to go. When I am faced with a challenge, I view it as a stepping-stone, and I continue to make steps towards my goals. During the moments when I feel like giving up, I remind myself of why I started. By doing so, I've developed resilience and learned how to overcome challenges and keep going. Now, keeping it going doesn't mean that I don't rest. I rest to re-energize and, at times, to re-strategize my plans and review what worked, what didn't work, and how I can make a better plan to achieve my goals.

I use a vision board as a tool to help me set and achieve my goals. A vision board, to me, is a visual representation of your goals. I believe when your goals are displayed it provides clarity and helps you to remain focus. In the center of my vison board is the word *Manifestation.* Around that word I chose four or five areas in my life that I wanted manifested and placed those areas on the vision board. Before I begin to look through magazines or the internet for pictures or words to put on the board of what I want my future to look like, I first visualize the future in my mind. I visualize myself achieving my goals and expressing emotions associated with what I have achieved. Next, I acknowledge where I am, where I plan to go, and how I plan to get there. Then I find ways to become the person in the vision by using the SMART business principle to help map out strategies. Vision boards are a great tool, but they don't work unless you work – you have to do the work. You can attend as many empowerment sessions, webinars, conferences, summits and download free content on how to start the business, but none of that will work unless you do the work.

If you are considering becoming an entrepreneur, I encourage you to '**Just Start**.' The beginning of the journey is challenging and unrewarding. However, you have to start somewhere.

Ask yourself, *what resources do you have that you can utilize and maximize to help you achieve your goals?* On the day I was given the inspiration to write my book, the resource that I already had was my knowledge on restoration. I grabbed a notepad and pen and sat in a quiet place and wrote up to ten pages. Today, whenever I am given a speaking opportunity, I walk with those ten pages to show people that you can start where you are with what you have.

My encouragement to you: -

1. Don't allow what you don't know or don't have access to, to stop you from pursuing your goals.
2. Identify people in your life that can help you achieve your goals and develop a support system of people who believe in you and your goals. Note, this support system may not include your family and friends.
3. On your journey, you will need to be vigilant. Extend your network by attending events and meeting people who have a similar interest in what you are working toward.

I appreciate the opportunity to write this article to share my journey with you. These three words—**Believe**, **Win**, and **Manifest**—have guided me on my journey and can help you in starting your journey as an entrepreneur.

1. **Believe** – Believe in who you are. First, you have to know who you are, and whose you are. You need to develop a belief system about yourself. Believe that you can do all things but focus on maximizing one strength at a time for greater results. Believe that it is possible for you to achieve everything you have made up in your mind to pursue. Believe that you have already achieved your goals. Move in the direction that you want your life to go, dress the part, join discussions online and offline that are in alignment with your plans for your life, attend events with the people you aspire to be among. Even when things don't look like they are going according to plan, you have to believe that it's working for your good and in your favor. You have to believe that you can design the life that you want! You have to believe that all things are possible! You have to believe in yourself!
2. **Win** – Develop a winning mindset! Against all odds, make winning your only option. You hold the key to your success, and you decide whether you win or lose. Winners don't make excuses; they take action. I accomplish my goals in life by obtaining tunnel vision. This simply means when I am focused on achieving a goal, I say no to anything that is not contributing to that goal to help me avoid distractions. I am disciplined and consistent in my actions to reach the finish line. I don't stop working when I am faced with a challenge; I

view the challenge as an opportunity, and I build endurance. I have experienced failures and setbacks along the entrepreneurial journey, but I don't allow the failures to keep me back. I maintain faith in my ability to win.

If you aspire to be an entrepreneur, I encourage you to define what winning means to you. My definition of winning is to achieve my goals without losing balance in life. Next, be resilient, you will need to know how to manage disappointments when things don't work out as you hoped. When this happens allow yourself to express the emotions that come with the disappointment and keep going. Re-strategize if you have you to, but keep going, review your strategy, and identify what worked and what didn't work but don't give up. Be consistent and be disciplined. Keep making steps toward your goals, develop a schedule to help keep you focused, and avoid distractions. A distraction is anything that takes your focus away from your goals. You have to develop an interest in yourself, and when you do this, you will know what is worth your time and your energy.

After you have decided which business venture you would like to explore, do your research. After I wrote my book, I needed a publisher. I started to look online, and I found a publisher who had very good reviews. I contacted the publishing company, submitted my manuscript, received a publishing contract and paid in full. I was excited as I was making strides to becoming a published author, or so I thought. I thought all publishing companies provided full editing services. Did you know there are different types of editing? Well, I didn't know that at the time and the publishing company I choose to work with didn't offer editing and it was a nightmare to obtain a refund. Do your research this will save you a lot of time, money, and mistakes.

3. **Manifest** – You can't be what you can't see. Speak what you want to see happen in your life and work towards that and ignore what's not in alignment with your goals. Take holistic steps toward your goals by aligning your spirit, body, and soul with what you want. Recite affirmations and make them a part of your lifestyle. Write out your affirmations for what you would like manifested in your life. I spend thirty minutes every morning visualizing my day and my life. I use affirmations to support my visualization. For example, if I want to be a speaker at an event, an affirmation to support the visualization would be, "*Today, I will receive an email asking to confirm my availability to speak at an event. At the event, the words that I speak will inspire women to be motivated. My knowledge coupled with my experience will positively impact and empower the lives of women attending event.*"

I have learnt to be present in the moment and enjoy my journey instead of constantly thinking about how far I have to go. I am grateful for the things that I have accomplished on my journey and the progress that I have made toward my goals. At the end of each week, I write down the things that I have accomplished along with what I am grateful for, and at the beginning of the following week, I read them. This has helped me get rid of limited beliefs about myself and increased my ability to succeed. I continue to surround myself with people who believe in me; my dreams; and my ability to believe, win, manifest and ultimately achieve my goals.

The journey is not easy, but in the end, if you stay focused, you will experience joy, growth, and success.

You too can become a successful businesswoman - Just Start.

Wilma Blyden is an author, speaker, and founder of the network **She Designed the Life She Wanted**. The network is aimed at women who are focused on self-improvement and are looking to design a meaningful, impactful, and joy-filled life. Wilma believes that biblically based principles are keys to creating a lifestyle of impact and teaches those principles to women to empower them.

She is the author of *She Designed the Life She Wanted - Four Women, Four Journeys, One Church*; this book shares the transparent story of four women and the challenges they faced on their Christian journey and how they used biblically based principles to overcome those challenges.

She regularly hosts and speaks at workshops, retreats, conferences, and other events. If you would like your audience to be inspired and equipped with knowledge on creating a lifestyle of impact, book Wilma to speak at your next event.

Nothing Pays Off Without Commitment and Focus

Corinthian Carouthers

Many people don't feel accomplished in life because of the dreams and goals they have yet to achieve. You may have goals of writing a book, losing weight, making a six-figure income, starting your own business and becoming your own boss, BUT DON'T QUIT! I have encountered many obstacles and challenges. If being committed and focus had not played a part in my journey, I would have folded many years ago.

In 1999, I opened Creative Hair School of Cosmetology (an 8,000 square feet beauty school) located in Flint, Michigan. My background did not include a college education, but it did include beauty school training and a will to pursue my dreams. Without a college degree, I was afraid my journey would be difficult.

When opening a business such as a beauty school, there are certain ordinances you have to get through to be approved in that community. Trying to get the business open was one of the biggest challenges. The township I was working with gave me a difficult time.

One board member asked me, "Why do you want to open a school? You people open salons." That comment could have stopped me and even made me believe that what I was trying to do was unattainable. No insurance companies would bond me. After countless meetings and visits with the state and township, I was finally able to open my beauty school.

Now that my beauty school was open and running, the challenges began. Beauty school isn't just about making people look and feel good, although that is a result of training. Beauty school is an educational institution, and it takes a good team and personnel to help bring dreams to life. Being a young minority woman business owner, I believed that the people around me were in support of my dreams of helping women and men become self-sufficient entrepreneurs. However, I later learned that the people I hired to help cultivate the lives of the people we were educating were trying to get the beauty school closed. Reports of complaints were sent to the State with inaccurate information. That taught me a lot about the hearts of people. Not everyone has your best interest at heart. But that did not stop me.

I made the news when another local beauty school tried to set fire to my school in fear of their students attending my school.

In 2004, I was diagnosed with a brain tumor. It was devastating. I had the tumor removed after a 10-hour surgery. The doctors told my family that it did not look good for me, but my life was spared through the grace of God. I had given years of my life in pursuit of helping others pursue theirs. In sight of that, I lost sight of self-care. Everything had been about the business.

Once I recovered from the surgery, I was back at it. Yes, there were many bumps still ahead. I couldn't pay my bills, got $10,000 behind in rent, no support from family and friends, had to move in with my daughter, while going 12 years without a paycheck. I have a true friend Cheryl who went five years without a paycheck, and there was Jackqline who also stayed in the fight with me.

My journey has been a rough one, leading me down roads that were hard, bumpy, wide, and narrow. Years later, my marriage of 28 years was in danger and soon later led to divorce. Out of all the obstacles I faced, my life partner of 28 years was no longer in this fight with me. The pain was difficult at times, but I made sure to keep my eye on the prize and keep my vision before me. When times got hard, I knew that the rewards would be worth it, and having the faith is what kept me strong in difficult times.

Times have been hard, but times have been great also. I have been blessed with two children who are co-owners of the beauty school, and that has made all my hard work and sacrifice worth it. I birthed the dream, and they are carrying it on. Not many African-American businesses are second generation. We are blessed to be able to do this together.

When my children joined the business, they brought so much liveliness and creativity and great energy to the atmosphere. This is year 20 for the beauty school, and my heart is thrilled.

As a family business, we have had our difficult times and surprising moments together. Right when we were repositioning the business and getting ready to rebrand it, a nationally known beauty school came into the area and took over the market. Many of our students transferred, and some clients joined them. It was a blow to our business and our morale, but together as a family, we were committed to the dream and dedicated to our focus. For eight years, we were in competition with that beauty school that had 72 locations in 50 states. After eight years of being in the area and our #1 competition, the school closed without notice. We had been preparing the business as if they did not exist, and when they closed, we gained their students and clients. We did not let them being here cause us to grow weary or give up. We did not doubt ourselves or our business.

The beauty school has sustained through the Flint Water Crisis. We serviced Flint residents to free hair care services through our community based program "Free Care For Your Hair." We have given over $350,000 in scholarships to students who were unable to fund their way through beauty school.

Through my commitment and focus, the beauty school has graduated 100s of students in the areas of cosmetology, esthetics, manicuring, instructors training, and natural hair care. These students have become licensed and are doing great things in the industry. Creative Hair School is also the only school in the State of Michigan that offers a Natural Hair Cultivation program. This program teaches proper cultivation in natural hair care, styling, and braiding.

In 2018, another obstacle came unexpectedly. After being in the location I had been in for 19 years, I received a letter stating I had to move in 30 days. I could not believe what was happening. How was I going to move a beauty institution that is governed by the state and federal government in 30 days? How are the students and staff going to feel about this unexpected change? The location I was in had been purchased by a company that wanted my location for a marijuana manufacturing facility. My family and I looked and looked for a good location. We were blessed to obtain the prime location of our prior competitor, including all the equipment and furniture. We purchased the facility that was built to perfection for a beauty school.

Today, all my struggles and sacrifices have been worth it. I have an amazing team who are passionate about their work and dedicated to the students' success. I have two amazing children who are growing the business like never before, and I have my life in which I am able to enjoy through the grace of God.

Recently, I've been featured as one of the top 25 Women in Business in *Courageous Woman Magazine*. I have received some amazing awards, shared speaking engagements with some elite people, and impacted lives on a daily basis. I am also proud to say I have never taken out any loans from a bank or financial institution.

This would have never happened if commitment and focus did not take place. Commitment and focus have to be a daily routine. If I can follow you and see how you spend your day and time, I will see what you are committed to. Commitment is simply dedication, loyalty, faithfulness, and being obligated to your given cause. Three keys you want to remember:

1. Without commitment, nothing happens.
2. You cannot conquer what you are not committed to.

3. Motivation is what gets you started, but commitment is what keeps you going.

Focus involves the ability to pay attention to the things that distract you.

F.O.C.U.S. Focus On Commitment Until Satisfied

Being in business will not be easy, but staying focused and committed is what pays off.

For the past 20 years, **Corinthian Carouthers** has owned and operated her own beauty school, Creative Hair School of Cosmetology. Her school provides services to the public in the areas of hair, skin, and, nails for a fraction of salon prices.

Ms. Carouthers' school offers training in Cosmetology, Esthetician, Nails, and Instructor's Training. She is very proud to be the only school that offers a Natural Hair Braiding Academy in the state of Michigan. The Academy teaches techniques and braiding styles such as zillions, corn-rolls, locs, loc-twist, kinky-twist, and goddess braids. The classes are taught by her daughter Corinthian Carouthers II, 11, who is also a licensed cosmetologist.

Her beauty school is accredited through N.A.C.C.A.S. and the U.S. Dept. of Education. Her students have participated in competitions in hair shows, hair wars and Bronner's Brothers. Her school has graduated hundreds of students, and she celebrates them for their endurance by giving a cap and gown ceremony. Many have become licensed, self-sufficient, and have gone on to do great things in the beauty industry by opening up their own salons and becoming master educators, instructors, platform artists, and beauty coaches.

Corinthian loves her community and has given out over $350,000 in scholarships and serviced hundreds of clients for the Free Care For Your Hair event due to the city's "lead in water" crisis. She has been a guest speaker and has recently been featured as one of the top 25 Women in Business in *Courageous Woman Magazine.*

On Facebook, you can learn more about Ms. Carouthers and her work (handles: CreativeHairSchool and Corinthian Carouthers).

Harnessing the Power to S.E.R.V.E.™

Taking a Leap of Faith…Journey of Redefining What's Possible

Gail M. Carter

Many people are afraid to take a leap of faith…to take the big plunge to start a new journey in life. Many are caught in the trap of indecision. Many can feel stuck, stressed, and burned out, and they can crave more meaning, more impact but don't know how to strategically break free and level-up. A few years ago, I decided to reinvent my life and find my natural flow, something I enjoyed doing every day.

I am a corporate professional who turned entrepreneur and became founder and CEO of LightShift360, LLC with focus on leadership development and operational excellence. I am passionate about inspiring high-achieving professionals to get the most out of life, find meaning, grow and increase maximum performance by harnessing the power to S.E.R.V.E.™ so they can effectively lead others and create even more impact and fulfillment in their lives, businesses, and communities. **S.E.R.V.E.™** is our unique **5-Step-Methodology**: 1-**S**-Strategic Planning to Maximize Success, 2-**E**-Empowering Mindset to Fulfill Dreams, 3-**R**-Responsible Action to Create Results, 4-**V**-Values

Leadership to Make a Difference, and 5-**E**-Expanding Reach to Maximize Impact.

I am originally from the tiny Caribbean island of Barbados. I went to the same high school, Combermere, as popular singer Rhianna. I appreciate my global experiences. I first traveled internationally at 10 years old. Over time, I have traveled to 20 countries and 4 continents. I moved to the USA at 18 to pursue my undergraduate degree in civil engineering. I later earned two master's degrees in business (MBA) and international development and social policy.

I successfully climbed the corporate ladder at Fortune 500 companies and created opportunities that led to promotions to various management positions in civil engineering, business, and project management for billion-dollar projects in the oil/gas/solar industry. I will always be grateful for the supervisors I have had during my career. Entrepreneurship is a roller coaster with unpredictable ups and downs. My corporate experience taught me the importance of business planning, discipline, logical-problem-solving skills, integrity and accountability; how to work under pressure; the ability to effectively delegate, get buy-in from others; create structures, systems, processes, and automations to improve efficiencies; and the art of networking with influential people. I think our journey and past experiences help us to get from one point to another in life.

My Inspiration to Pursue Entrepreneurship

I wanted to play an infinite game in life. It took about a year of strategic planning, preparation, and mindset to advance beyond my 9-5 job. Though externally, I had a successful career and education, I still felt internally unfulfilled. I felt I reached a ceiling. What was missing was a sense of purpose, impact, and fulfilling something bigger than myself. I wanted the freedom, balance, flexibility, more autonomy and self-expression to powerfully create and make a bigger difference in society. I enjoy helping people to level-up and creating new possibilities. I had to redefine my definition of success from short-term thinking like (i) how much money I was making, (ii) my ego…looking good versus looking bad, and (iii) having a prestigious career, to a new paradigm of longer-term thinking about the legacy I want to leave in this world. At LightShift360, LLC we offer workshops like "How to Unlock Your Potential Daily," live events like "Renewal360 Encounter" and global leadership retreats, "Renewal360 Caribe." Our online products include "Impact360 Leadership System" as well as published books. We offer 1-on-1 private and group leadership and personal development coaching programs. We are available for speaking engagements for your organization.

Becoming a National Speaker and Best-Selling Author

These are excellent communication platforms. Someone needs to hear our journey. By sharing these, we create hope and inspire others to be better. I had the opportunity to speak and teach internationally in Central America. My first book was *5,000 Smiles To Happiness - 5 Steps to Renew Your Mind, Revive Your Joy and Unleash Your Leadership Potential.* I also co-authored Amazon Best Seller *Speaking My Truth* anthology and

The Making of a Successful Business Woman. I recently hosted my own live event, Renewal360 Encounter, in Tampa, FL, and I was a speaker at the inaugural SpeakerCon 2019 Conference in Washington, DC, hosted by Dr. Cheryl Wood. I also spoke at the 7th Annual Leading Within Conference, in Washington, DC. My goal is to speak on more international stages in the next couple years.

Why Some People Don't Start Businesses

People are afraid of change and taking risks. Many think that because you leave your job to start your own company, that life is great because you are your own boss. Yes, you have more freedoms, but it sure takes lot of work to really launch a company, and it takes a lot of commitment, dedication, focus and a lot of structure to really stay committed also. My perspective is how would I feel about it later in life if I looked back and I never took the opportunity. I reflected on my past successful life and reaffirm that **"I'm already a winner in life!"** I believe more on betting on myself versus holding on to scarcity and finite mindset or give into fear or the impostor syndrome. I must believe and bet on myself simply because I can create my own story and my own reality. You can live the life that you are called to live. Refuse to allow fear and stories that you create in your own mind to stop that from happening. I find hiring a coach, surrounding myself with positive people, praying, and reciting affirmations daily also help keep positive flow state.

Outside of fear, having money and cash flow is another reason that stops people. Startup costs for businesses and entrepreneurs are a lot. But how do you stomach that, right? I really believe, and this was a total mindset shift, because we are all programmed that were supposed to pay down debt, not spend and hold onto everything, that holding onto everything holds us back. I had to recreate a new mindset to realize the same corporations that I was working for all those years also borrowed money to invest in their businesses. It's called leverage. It's a positive thing. You must build business credit; you must spend money to make money. All these things are true. Millionaires do the same thing. It's just the power of leverage.

My Advice for New Entrepreneurs

Follow these short snippets from our the 5-Step-Methodology S.E.R.V.E.™ Blueprint under our Impact360 Leadership System to harness your inner power to create even more impact.

S-Strategic Planning to Maximize Success: You need a plan to successfully accomplish your goals. A simple 1-page business plan is ideal. In the beginning, it's important to self-reflect and understand your strengths and how to compliment your weaknesses. Planning for alternate sources of funding is also important and so having solid personal or business credit is helpful to be able to borrow capital for the business.

E-Empowering Mindset to Fulfill Dreams: The early stage start-up life can be stressful and unbalanced. We work much longer hours than the typical 9-5, but we must enjoy what we do. We must believe in our purpose and find balance. The miracles happen during the commitment, faith and sharing the journey with others. Continue to learn and grow, get a coach and an accountability partner, and be sure not to burn out too early.

R-Responsible Action Plans to Create Results: Unlike the overly cautious personality that I had while working in corporate America, as an entrepreneur, I must take more risks and test things to see if they work. In the beginning, there are so many new hats to wear, marketing, branding, legal, accounting. Hire a part-time virtual assistant to help with the day-to-day administration. Use online freelancers to help with branding and marketing, and hire a consultant to help with bookkeeping and legal structures. We can't do everything on our own, and it is important to be able to delegate to others and inspire others to get behind our vision and mission.

V-Values Leadership to Make a Difference: Understand the value that you bring and the viability of the market. Build something you believe in and are passionate about that also aligns with your values. Focus on the legacy that you want to have in this world.

E-Expanding Reach to Maximize Impact: Get out of the office and network and serve others. People will get to know you and learn about your services. Also, staying in the office can get quite lonely. Find opportunities to be in the room as your new connections can also be great referrals. Be yourself. Push past the status quo. Don't be afraid of change, or what others think. Take risks and bet on yourself.

The life we want is waiting…take the first step. Instantly connect with me on social media **#GailMCarter** and **#LightShift360** and by **texting "GAIL" to 64600** to get my **digital business card** to your phone. Schedule a FREE discovery call there. Learn more at **gailmcarter.com** and **lightshift360.com** to hire us for training and speaking engagements.

Gail M. Carter is the founder of LightShift360, LLC. Gail develops workplace leadership and personal development programs that lead to even more engagement, growth, profit, and purposeful contributions to society. She held various management positions in infrastructure, electric power, and renewable energy during her 16-year career in corporate America. A licensed engineer, she holds an M.B.A. in business administration, M.A. in international development, and a B.S. in civil engineering. Gail has traveled to 20 countries and 4 continents, and actively volunteers internationally. She is a speaker, an author and was the recipient of the "Woman to Watch" Award for leadership and volunteerism.

Move Using God's Plan

Dr. Cortesha Cowan

I love being a serial entrepreneur.

I got my first taste of entrepreneurship when I was a young girl. I grew up around entrepreneurship as my grandparents owned their own restaurant. I watched so many of their friends own businesses as well. My grandma instilled inside of us entrepreneurship, and I had a sneak peek of it by always working after school at the restaurant.

I decided to become a business owner after I saw so many women in my medical school not being able to graduate because of a lack of childcare, and in 2005, I sought to open my very first childcare center. The goal was to open one close to the school because this would fix the problem for the women who needed childcare. This could help them finish their medical degrees. Little did I know this was the start of entrepreneurship for me.

My business has evolved significantly since then, but I'm so grateful for the way I started.

One of my most successful businesses today is my nonprofit organization Mothers Helping Mothers, which was birthed in 2007. This isn't my most successful business because it is a multi-million dollar company. It's not. It's my most successful because it has helped over 22,000 lives since the day it open, from housing to childcare support, to case management services, to mentoring and just watching these young teen moms evolve, has made it the most successful thing that I have ever started.

I have successfully gone from that to selling my services on how to open a childcare center, how to open a home for the homeless—becoming an amazing birthing business coach for my clients. I have also become a best-selling author with my co-authors in several books, and now, I am a solo author for a book to help you find your purpose and passion in life and make the best journey for yourself. On top of these wonderful things, I am a sought-out speaker for events, retreats, and workshops. I now teach how to turn your services into a product. This has significantly scaled my businesses.

I love what I do. It brings so much joy to my heart to be an entrepreneur that also gives back. I love being someone that the young girls can look up to. To know that even as a former teen mom myself and the trials that I went through in life made me a trailblazer for generations to come. Being a female entrepreneur is not easy, but it is worth the journey. It is worth leaving a legacy for your children and your children's children. For the last 20 years, there have been some good days and some bad days as an entrepreneur, but the good days definitely outweigh the bad days as there's so much I am thankful for.

For those of you with the entrepreneurial spirit, I offer the following pieces of advice to consider.

Stay connected with the source that gives you strength and endurance. Another facet of my success is that I have stayed connected with my spiritual side and with hearing from God. I'm in the kingdom business, which makes this more of a rewarding journey for me. I allow God to continue to be my guide. And my teacher. Therefore, I have such an amazing journey. I know all my life accomplishments and success is because of Him.

Use your passion and purpose for success. Consider those things you are passionate about and reflect on how those passions connect with your life's purpose. Might one of these connections (or more) make for a successful business? I learned how to turn my passion and purpose into something more driven that will help others achieve their entrepreneurship goals.

Know your market. If you don't know where your market is and what they want, it will make things much harder.

Set goals you can handle. It is great to have big dreams and big visions, but those dreams and visions are often achieved through the successes of small goals.

Let your personal tribe love you during the journey. I am blessed to have a supporting husband and family who stands right beside me.

Let your business tribe love, comfort, and advise you during the journey. I have a community of like-minded female entrepreneurs who I can go to when business gets tough for me.

Be patient. Always remember that success is not going to happen overnight.

Have a mentor. As a business owner, you will do a lot of things to get your business running, but if you can find someone who is already where you're trying to go, it will be a huge benefit to you as they can offer advice that may get you where you want to be with fewer bumps along the journey.

Follow your gut. Sometimes, we let the fear of failure keep us from pursuing goals, but if you had that gut feeling to do something—try it. What's the worst that's going to happen? You're going to make a mistake and move on. The best success has been from learning from my mistakes and persevering through them.

Hold fast to your vision. Do not let people dictate what it is that you see for your vision, and regarding your vision, please make sure you understand your "Why" before getting started.

Remain focused. And while being focused realize that your vision grows yearly the more you tap into your passion and what it is that you see for yourself. Your focus might change because of this growth.

Be a lifelong learner. Being open to learning is vital to success, too. As a purpose-driven entrepreneur and author, I spend so much time learning and growing. I am driven by my passion and purpose not by my pocket and how much money I'm making.

Be persistent. One thing I have never done is give up. Call me the Perseverance Queen because I will try and try until I'm where I'm supposed to be. Giving up is not an option for me, and it shouldn't be an option for you.

Remember why you started. When I first started this journey, I remember my energy being through the roof! I had so many ideas coming to mind. It was exciting and encouraging. It's important to remember those early-day moments of joy. Even on the days you don't feel like doing the work, remember Day One and rekindle that energy. I've never treated my business like a hobby because we often give up hobbies without even thinking about them.

Provide self-care. One of the greatest things about being an entrepreneur happens when I have an opportunity to go speak or attend a book signing for a book that was released, and I get to take my husband along with me. It's being able to blend my personal life and needs with my business life. Remember to keep a life outside of work. It is so easy to make the mistake of not having self-care; I have learned the hard way, and it is something I have now incorporated it into my monthly calendar. Self-care and entrepreneurship go hand-in-hand. Life will happen, and when it does, it can be very hard to run your business. Please find a way to separate your business from your personal life and plan for times like these. We can have "life happening" without our business crumbling.

Manage your time. This ties into providing self-care. Remember that you are more than a business owner, and it's important to balance your time in the business and in your personal life. Setting boundaries with my business and personal life became HUGE for me in 2019. I personally don't work weekends or after 8 p.m. most days, and my clients know and respect that. It took me three years to get here, however. Going into 2020, I will be making it my business to have even more personal time. "I am not any good for you if I'm burned out" is my new model. I am still purpose-driven, but as an entrepreneur, I (and you, too) have to really set some great boundaries in my life, and I plan to make 2020 the best year yet for me as an entrepreneur.

I am blessed to be a part of this book collaboration to give you just a little inspiration for you as you embark upon this amazing journey of entrepreneurship. I pray that you have enjoyed this chapter and that you have been able to see inside my world just a little bit and learn that entrepreneurship, with its ups and downs, is one of the greatest things that you can accomplish in life (for me, outside of being a child of God, a wife, a mother, a daughter, a sister, a niece, and an aunt).

Good luck and God bless.

Dr. Cortesha Cowan is known as "Dr. Coach Cowan" for her ability to help women and teen girls grow their confidence and passion. She has built a step-by-step system model for opening homes for teen mothers that are homeless or in foster care.

As the founder and CEO of Mothers Helping Mothers Inc., this vision expanded to providing safe shelter and food in Cape Town South Africa in 2019. Our ultimate goal is to break the generational cycle of teen pregnancy.

Dr. Cowan has received countless awards including a lifetime achievement award in 2016 from the 44th President Barack Obama. Dr. Cowan has spent the last

13 years helping others to find what they are called on this earth to do.

To stay connected with Dr. Cowan, you can search *Dr. Cortesha Cowan* on all social media platforms, or you can view her website: www.drcorteshacowan.com.

From Twos and Fews to Six Figures: How I Shifted My Side Hustle to a Successful Business

Shuntai Hill

"Success is not the absence of failure; it's the persistence through failure."
Aisha Tyler

Since I was a child, I dreamed of being an entrepreneur. In the early '80s, my cousins and I would twist head bands from our hair yarn and sell them to the neighbors or at our parents' weekend card parties. I've always had the love of being a business woman.

Over the years, my business ideas evolved; my ex-husband and I sold baseball caps and jerseys, party planning, selling college textbooks on Amazon, and life coaching just to name a few. Some were failures—others small successes.

All of my businesses had one thing in common. They were all side hustles. Nothing to be taken too seriously. They weren't bad hustles because I made a few dollars. However, most of my energy was focused on my raising a family, working full time, and being a full-time college student.

My real passion in business was ignited when I hit my fork in the road in 2013. My youngest son was graduating from high school, and my dreams of being an empty nester was abruptly halted when I learned my mother could no longer live alone due to early onset Alzheimer's. I was in graduate school pursuing a graduate degree in professional counseling and somewhat content with my corporate job.

I made the decision to move home with my mother to care for her. Being her only child, there was no other choice. However, understanding the depth of my mother's reality made me reflect on my life. The key to my peace and happiness would be connected to my passion. I just needed to find it. So, I went on a quest of self-discovery; I read self-help books, attended seminars for women, joined social groups, and spent time with family. The path to discovery led me to helping others deal with life adversities through counseling.

In 2015, again, I found myself at another fork in the road. I was preparing to graduate with a degree in counseling, and I was planning on opening a private practice, Re-Connect My Life Counseling. My only problem: I had over 13 years on my job. I was vested, and it was consistent pay. Things weren't perfect, but I was managing my life rather well.

Unfortunately, that's all I was doing was managing. I was on autopilot. Not truly loving my life, just watching it pass by. I became uncomfortable in my profession. My desire was to be my own boss and help people at the same time. I wanted to control my income and stop the game of waiting for someone to give me a raise each year. My passion was bubbling inside of me, and I needed to make some serious decisions. I could no longer ignore my destiny of helping others. Over the years, I had gone through so many ups and downs and managed to keep my sanity. Therefore, my goal was to open my own private counseling practice after graduation.

I began to romanticize about being my own boss: more time with family, unlimited income, being able to take luxury vacations, coming and going as I please, etc. " Life would be perfect"... "I would love every minute of it"—I thought this was going to be awesome.

I wanted to make this dream a reality. The same month I graduated with my master's in counseling, I opened my private practice, Re-Connect My Life Counseling. I rented a small two room office suite in downtown Flint and continued working my corporate job during the day. I was seeing two or three clients a week, if I was lucky. Working with clients made me happy. However, my happiness was not paying the bills. Again, I found myself at another fork in the road. How can I do what I love and be financially stable at the same time?

I decided that if I am going to work in my passion, then I needed to go in 100%. I needed to stop treating my love of counseling like a side hustle. It had to become my main priority, but I couldn't just up and quit my job. That would be financially irresponsible. I had too many people depending on me. I needed to be strategic. So, I gave myself six months to save more money, pay off debts, grow my business, and plan my corporate exit.

Unfortunately, life happened and things did not go as perfectly as planned. Everything that could have went wrong, went wrong. I began having issues on my job, my mother passed away from complications of Dementia, my sons were experiencing difficulties in their lives, my fiancé was battling congestive heart failure. My life was chaotic. Despite it all, I clutched on to my passion. It was part of my peace. I desired it more than ever. Experiencing others deal with their mortality made my heart yearn to fulfill my promise to myself. I thought more about my legacy. What do I want to be remembered for? What can I leave for my children and granddaughter? How can I be a blessing to others?

Shift happens, and it can propel us away from our path or keep us on it. I had to change my mindset. I will no longer allow the things beyond my control to break me. In the spring of 2017, I left my corporate job and went into practice full time. During this time, I reunited with my father, became a grandmother, married my best friend, traveled out of the country, and expanded my business. My mother must have thought about her legacy to me. She invested into my life on so many levels. My practice is no longer just a two room office suite. I own a 1,400 sq. ft. building with 13 clinicians. I've expanded the Group Practice into Metro Detroit. I am not saying this to brag. My journey was not easy, and it continues to have its struggles, but I fought for it all. To be the Boss, I have sacrificed time with family, could not take vacations, worked long days, and decreased my income several times.

People see me now and assume that I've always had it together, and that is the furthest from the truth. I am a woman who is constantly evolving. I hurt, I love, I cry, and I work hard. I learned that it was never about being the Boss. It's not about being perfect. It was about gaining control of my destiny, living in my truth, and fighting tooth and nail to maintain it. It was about never giving up on my passion. My life continues to be imperfect. I continue to experience challenges, and I realize no matter how much money you make or how many businesses you own, challenges will always show up unexpectantly. It's part of life.

My dream became my reality with a few edits. I worked long days because I wanted my business to grow. I sacrificed in the short term because I had a vision of the long term. Re-Connect My Life, Inc. is now a six-figure business making an impact in the communities we serve. I am amazed by my staff and their commitment because I could not continue at this level by myself.

This is how I was able to turn my practice into a six-figure business:

1. Stop treating your passion like a side hustle. At some point, it needs to become your priority.
2. Learn that a little fear can be beneficial. It has the power to push you toward greatness, but too much of it can cause one to be stagnant.
3. Love your passion unconditionally. Loving what you do allows one to deal with the shifts along the way.
4. Learn to say "No" to some things to make room for things that really matter.
5. Be consistent with healthy behavior. No one likes inconsistency. Being consistent with

healthy behavior increases patterns of good behavior.

6. Keep your word. No one likes a liar, nor do you want to be perceived as one. Employees, colleagues, friends, and community partners will respect you more.
7. Find balance. Too much work or too much pleasure can be detrimental to your mental, physical, and spiritual health.
8. Take care of yourself. If you don't care for yourself, it will be difficult to sustain yourself, a business, or family.
9. Sacrifice. You won't always be in a position to do everything you want. Small sacrifices along the way will pay off later.
10. Invest in your passion. Always be open to learning more and staying in the forefront of your expertise. Attend conferences, trainings, network with others in your field, and read.
11. Keep a good support system. It's important to have positive and supportive people in your corner.
12. Learn to be a good communicator.

Ms. Shuntai Hill is a nationally certified counselor. She is the CEO of Re-Connect My Life, Inc. providing mental health counseling for depressive, anxiety, and sexual disorders. A published author and media contributor, Ms. Hill's works appear in several major media outlets. She is also the host of *On the Couch with Shuntai & Friends*.

You can learn more about Ms. Hill and her work at her website: www.re-connectmylife.com.

The Miseducation of a College Graduate

Dr. Ladel Lewis

The late great Malcolm X once said, "Education is the passport to the future. For tomorrow belongs to those that prepare for it today." That quote was recited as gospel throughout my high school years. Keeping that in mind, I decided to obtain my passport from some of the best public universities and received one of the highest degrees possible, a Doctor of Philosophy. The sky was the limit, and nothing could hold me back. Per society's standards, I was ready for the world. As a credentialed African American (Descendant of Slaves), I was told that I could write my own ticket anywhere with a Ph.D. The U.S. Census Bureau cosigned this by reporting less than 2% of all Americans have one. That makes me one in a million. My working-class parents were extremely proud of their first generation college graduate. I felt invincible walking across that stage. However, the feeling soon departed as I tried to redeem my "ticket" and claim my piece of the American Dream.

My stellar grade point average and dropping the name of my alma mater landed me nothing. I thought at least the dean would vouch for me because I always made his coveted list. This would not be the case. I continued to receive rejection letter after rejection letter. Some places may as well have said, "Tough luck," while many never had the courtesy to even follow-up. I felt deceived. Misled. I did everything right. I graduated high school, stayed out of trouble, went to college, and got great grades. I even ate my vegetables. This was not the future that society had promised me. Where did I go wrong? I did exactly as Brother Malcolm advised, or did I?

It was time to revisit Bro. Malcolm's quote and get a true understanding of what he meant. Of all the great classes I took, no one offered a class on likability and social capital. Many refer to this as "networking." Communication Theory, Public Speaking, and Interpersonal Communication sound good when you boastfully rattle them off, but how applicable are they? How transferable are they in the job market? In the interviewing process? In the referral process? The answer is "not very." I had to come up with a different plan of attack. To do this, a shift in my ideas about "schooling" had to take place.

The word "education" is a tricky word. Although many see it through the lens of an institution of higher learning, it is defined as "the development of the abilities of the mind." Using that definition as a framework, one can conclude that education is not exclusively reserved for the college or university, but it can take place anywhere and at any time. It became evident that although I had a couple of graduate degrees, I needed to become more educated. Educated in people and how to create genuine relationships with them. These relationships may materialize into some great friendships, and some may increase my chance for opportunity. I decided to get educated in Likability, a new area that focuses on being likable. What's the use of having 500 degrees when you can't find one person to hire you or to do business with you? Well, search no more. Here are six simple steps that helped me along my journey and promoted the establishment of genuine relationships.

Smile

You will attract more people with a smile instead of with the "Sour Patch Kids" face. When I moved to the Washington, DC area, this guy stopped me and asked, "You're not from here, are you? Bewildered, I shook my head no. He replied, "I know because the women in this area don't smile. They walk around with a chip on their shoulder." I thought, *That's not a good way to make a first impression.* Smiles are powerful and contagious. Try smiling at someone. I guarantee you that they will at least return a smirk. They just can't help it. You remember the old saying "It takes more muscles to frown than to smile"? Well, I don't know that to be true. But I AM quite certain that our smile will brighten up someone's day and make you more approachable. Say cheese!

Say No to False Promises

"We must do lunch." Those are the words made famous by people who have no intention of breaking bread with you or ever seeing you again. However, it's the "in-thing" to say. I met a lady while attending a sorority networking event. Our conversation was flowing, and she asked me for my contact information so we could "do lunch." We exchanged business cards.

I had reached out to her on multiple occasions, and I never received a response. Did she have to "ghost me"? Not at all. I wasn't desperate for a meal, nor does it look like I miss any. Face it, you don't have to eat lunch with everyone. It's ok. Wrap up the conversation with "It was good speaking with you" or "I'm looking forward to hearing great things about your business" and leave it there.

Compliment Others

Let's be honest, flattery gets you a lot of places, but sincerity is what keeps you there. Speak from a genuine place. Mean what you say and say what you mean. Telling someone "I love your hair" when you actually don't isn't a good way to build a healthy relationship. There is always something genuinely positive to say. Maybe the hairstyle isn't the best, but the color is amazing. Maybe they have on a unique piece of jewelry. Let's focus on those things.

Be Genuine (and take a genuine interest in people)

Many people want to know, "Do you like me or do you like what I can do for you?" Networking begins with establishing genuine relationships. Acquiring new clients and landing monumental business deals often takes place between people who have a rapport with one another. This reminds me of a networking event I attended. I met an interesting individual. I found out their daughter was a senior in high school. Upon graduating high school, I was the recipient of dozens of scholarships. After exchanging stories of the importance of scholarship money, I promised that I would forward them the scholarships that came across my desk. I did just that. They were beyond appreciative. From there, we established a great professional relationship, and they referred my business to potential clients every chance they got. Contrary to popular belief, it is not always about "selling yourself," but more about "being yourself." However, be ye not deceived; it is vital to know your product by heart when asked. Be prepared, but do not be in-person SPAM. No one likes SPAM. Be someone who is truly interested in building new relationships.

Don't Play Business Card Poker

Everyone wants to make a lasting impression. They want the person they are speaking with to call them and become a business client immediately! They can't remember you without you leaving your business card, right? Wrong. They remember you by establishing relationships, not by dealing your contact information to everyone like you are playing business card poker. You may feel like those cards are burning holes in your pocket, but again, resist the urge to be in-person SPAM. That will only get your card tossed on the ground or directly into the garbage. If they want it, they will ask for it. Period. Otherwise, save a tree and reserve it for someone who is interested in following up with you.

Be an Active Listener

Have you witnessed someone who was more anxious to talk than they were to listen? They were too concerned with speaking their piece instead of engaging in a meaningful dialogue. I used to be "that girl." I was so consumed with saying something profound that I lost sight of the dyadic interaction that could change my life. Moreover, you may come across as pushy, self-centered, and uninterested. I encourage you to learn what not to do from this type of behavior and refrain from imitating it.

Everyone has value. Everyone's value is different, but nevertheless, they are worth SOMETHING. It takes a courageous woman to realize that and treat everyone like a very important person. The late H. Jackson Brown states, "At the end of the day people won't remember what you said or did, they will remember how you made them feel." If you make them feel like they are the VIP of that moment and give them your genuine undivided attention, that interaction will be remembered for years to come. It may even change the course of your life.

Dr. Ladel Lewis is a best-selling author, international speaker, and likability expert. She is the managing editor and columnist for *Courageous Woman Magazine*. Her sweet spot is conducting informationals for entrepreneurs and those looking to enhance their social network. Dr. Lewis is known for helping local organizations with membership issues through her highly specialized "Recruitment, Retention and Reclamation" and "Communicating Throughout the Generations" workshops. She's served as keynote speaker for organizations such as Minority Access and the Department of Labor. She resides in the Washington D.C. Metropolitan area with her family.

Dr. Lewis' social media handle for Instagram, LinkedIn, and Twitter is *Ladel Lewis*. You can also visit her website: www.ladellewis.com.

Becoming a Successful Business Woman

Tina D. Lewis

So, how do you become a successful business woman?

It's Easy!
Really Simple!

NOT!

It takes Discipline, Consistency, Hunger, and Hard Work! I remember when I was a single, teenage mother and a full-time student, taking 21 units. Every summer, I would "pretend" I wanted a 40-hour-a-week job. I would interview and tell them exactly what every human resource director dreams of hearing, "I want to grow with the company, work hard, promote to the top, and be an asset to the team and your company as a whole."

When the fall season came, I simply came up with a credulous excuse of why I could no longer work. The "real" reason was the fall semester of school was starting. In the immediate, I needed money to pay bills and survive. However, my long term goal was to not only receive a degree but to receive it with honors at the top of my class. I knew in my gut that I was going to be successful but was indoctrinated to believe the only way to reach success was through the hands of education.

Upon graduating from the Keck School of Medicine at the University of Southern California as a physician assistant, I felt that there was something missing. Although the work was meaningful and rewarding, I wasn't fulfilled. The desire to help people "heal" and have a "greater quality of life" was still prevalent and unquenchable. I soon realized the healing I was commissioned to provide was not just physical but intellectual and financial as well.

I was consciously aware that I was destined for more, but I didn't know what the "more" looked like or exactly what it was. I started my first business called "I Squared" (Internet Intellect) in 1990. The internet was new and everyone was afraid of it. Find a need and fill it, right?! In the summer, I went to businesses and asked if I could give them a presence on the World Wide Web for a fee. The benefit would be that they would be "first" and receive brand recognition and traffic to their brick & mortar. It was successful. I charged businesses $500 and earned enough to provide in abundance for me and my daughter. The fall season approached, and once again, I had to refocus on my greater goal. In 1994, I established a housekeeping service by serendipity. At the time, I was employed at the Watts Health Clinic in South Central LA. The mom of one of the nurses cleaned my apartment for a pittance (because she knew I was a struggling student). When her duties were completed, she arrived at the clinic to return my house keys. I was at the beach. (The details and repercussions are in my book scheduled for release Summer 2020!) The nurses, doctors, and administrators assumed I had a maid and asked, "How much does she charge?" BINGO! My second entrepreneur endeavor "Happy Housekeeping" was birthed!

I had no business acumen and simply ran an ad in the Yellow Pages, and business began to boom! It was not my passion nor anything that I enjoyed. This was strictly for income. After I paid my bills (rent, utilities, daughter's tuition, etc.), I then reinvested every penny back into my business. Eventually, I got burned out of attending school and running a physically demanding business.

It was hard! I had no systems. No coach. No mentor. No expertise. No experience. Just me hustling. It had to be a much better way, but my knowledge was limited. I then began to rigorously search, hunt, and become intrigued with business, earning money, and profit/loss. No matter what the amount of money that was needed was, I could conjure up a business (product and/or service) and produce it. I began to invest in courses, classes, masterminds, and mentors. I devoured knowledge and voraciously read autobiographies of the wealthy and emulated the people I studied. I spent more money than I ever earned, and I eventually grew. I took the blue pill and became fearless. I took major risks. I won. I conquered, and I also failed and took major losses.

Today, I have an extremely successful business strategy and social media marketing firm. I coach entrepreneurs on how to earn insanely more money, create time freedom where they are not slaves to the grind, and live a life they've only seen on *Lifestyles of the Rich and Famous.* I simply implement coveted systems that are used by billionaires that alone have allowed me to gross over a quarter-million dollars in six months. I totally believe that in order to create a business that is independent of you and to earn money while you sleep, you MUST automate and leverage the power of social media. I've invested hundreds of THOUSANDS of dollars on personal development, technology, systems, and mentorship so I could become the Expert and master the skillsets needed to become and remain a successful businesswoman. There are numerous entrepreneurs who are still doing things the "old" way, working ridiculous hours "IN" their business instead of "on" their business and becoming burned out or desperate that the money that they deserve evades them.

Listen, I don't know how to make gumbo (even though I love it!). I can't cook from scratch (don't have the patience). I have never done it or even desire to. I can't even tell you how to set the table properly, but what I can give you are the ingredients to being a successful businesswoman (or man!), and that will allow you to build a sustainable legacy and your seed to eat forever. PERIOD!

Here are the ingredients:

1. DESIRE - Do you have the inclination to be successful in business? To put in 10,000 hours to become an expert or a master?
2. ENTHUSIASM - Are you excited about the product, service, or information that you offer? Are you enthused about sharing it with others, the results that one receives or the value proposition that you bring to the marketplace?
3. CONSISTENCY/DISCIPLINE - Will you master the mundane and do it over and over and over and over and over again?
4. WORK ETHIC - Will you work hard and keep the goal/objective at the forefront of your mind? Will you do whatever is necessary no matter how you feel?
5. RESILIENCY - Will you be willing or have the proclivity to withstand or overcome challenges, difficulties and bounce back? Will you have that bulldog tenacity that no matter what happens, you win?
6. HUMILITY /COACHABILITY- No matter how much knowledge you've attained or money you've earned, will you be humble enough to seek help, ask for advice, be willing to learn, listen and leverage the expertise of others (even if their ideologies and methodologies are different from your own)?
7. NETWORK - Are you willing to collaborate, partner, create strategic alliances, and crosspollinate with others who have your same

demographics, but more importantly your core values, ethics and operate with integrity?

I know without a shadow of a doubt and can say it without any hesitation, the above is the recipe for becoming a wildly successful businesswoman. When you take those ingredients, Mix, Stir, and Blend with your God-given talent and Supernatural Favor, Bake for a period of time (the time of your success is totally dependent on you), take it out of the oven (there will be moments of extreme heat where you will want to quit, throw in the towel, disappear, but don't you dare. You were made and equipped for this!), and let it sit to cool (when your business is eventually on autopilot because you've heeded my advice and automated and delegated your business so that it runs without your participation), then Serve your gift to the world, you, my friend, are a Successful Business Woman!

I would be remiss not to share how to get started properly, so here are a few building blocks:

- Name your business AND purchase the domain name (and your name, too!)
- Get a website (even if it's a 1 pager)
- Register your business with the Secretary of State (LLC, C-Corp or S-Corp)
- Get an EIN (Employer ID#)/Tax ID: Free from IRS.gov
- Open a Business Bank Account (only $100 deposit needed)

There's so much more, and my contact is below to give you the launching pad (or Relaunching pad) to catapult your business to a 6 Figure Entity and beyond!

Remember: Rome wasn't built in a day, and it's not how you start but how you finish!

Please follow me on your favorite and most used social media platform:

- LIKE my Facebook Business Page Tina D. Lewis @6FigureGuru
- FOLLOW me on IG @tinadlewis
- SUBSCRIBE to my YouTube Channel
- FOLLOW me on Twitter @TinaDLewis
- Connect with me on LinkedIn @TinaDLewis
- FOLLOW me on Pinterest @TinaDLewis
- FOLLOW me on Tik Tok @Tina D. Lewis

Or, simply just call (310.496.5875 office) or email me (coachme@RoyaltyCoaching.com)!
Being!

How My Ex Inspired My Booming Interior Design Business

Knetta Lilly

It's been said some relationships are for a season, and some are for a lifetime. My relationship with my ex can be classified as both: a season for the relationship and a lifetime for the business.

My design business was inspired by my ex-boyfriend, Gary Ladler in 2002 while living in Houston. We met while he was working at Home Depot. I needed help with faux wood blinds, and although he worked in lighting, he somehow made his way over and introduced himself. Gary ended up being the handyman for my first home. Our business relationship evolved, and we began dating in March of 2002. Gary visited my home often and would compliment some aspect of my home décor during each visit. Sometimes, he complimented window treatments; other times, it would be the wall art. Other occasions, it might be the layering of textures and patterns throughout the home. After three months of dating, he made the most profound statement, and that statement changed my life forever.

Gary mentioned, "You have an awesome talent for home decorating, and you need to stop doing work for your friends for free. People will PAY good money for your services." Gary knew that I was helping friends with their homes, and he knew that I was not being paid for that work. Gary believed in my skills so much that he helped formulate my first business name, Diva-Designed Elegance. After creating the name, we obtained my business license, ordered business cards, and he professionally photographed my design projects to establish my portfolio. He provided candid insight on how to establish my vendor contact list for products and services. Gary would also provide handyman services for some of my client projects. I still don't know how Gary had so much knowledge about how to build this business when he wasn't a businessman himself, but he was the catalyst to building my brand until we broke up in 2007 when I moved to Atlanta for a job in the financial services industry. Although our relationship was only for a season of five years, Gary planted the seed for a lifetime of me pursuing my passion and sharing my gift with the world. I can't imagine my life without being able to create unique and beautiful spaces for others.

Once I moved to Atlanta, I didn't know ANYONE, so I kept my business in relative obscurity. I recall being in Atlanta for less than a month when I decided to order new business cards. I asked myself, "Why are you ordering business cards when you just moved across country for a new job?" I felt that God clearly spoke to me in that moment and said, "That job got you here, but your business is going to blow up here." With that revelation, I knew God had big things in store for me although I had no clue how my business would evolve. The scriptures say, "Faith without works is dead," so I believed in God's promises and began to grow my business organically. First, I changed my business name to my given name as I believed my name represented what I wanted my business to be: high-end, chic, and unique. The new business name was *K. Lilly Interiors, LLC.*

When I purchased a home in Atlanta in November 2008 and began decorating it, my coworkers who had become really close friends by now, marveled at the uniqueness of my design, requested my design assistance with their homes, and in turn, referred me to their friends for similar design services. I recall a coworker complimenting my work and saying, "You are really good....why do you work here? I shouldn't even know you because your work is on a whole different level." I've always been less than confident about my design skills, so I never bragged on what others called my "gift." I never felt that I was good enough simply because I didn't have any formal decorating and design training nor did I have any prestigious ASID (American Society of Interior Designers) certifications behind my name. I have since learned that your gift will make room for you, and God will make provision for you in unexpected ways.

My design business grew on word-of-mouth referrals, and I found that to be the best form of advertisement for my business. Nobody in Atlanta knew who I was as a designer, so I started building that notoriety. My home was featured in the *AJC Private Quarters*, and two of my clients' homes were also featured in the *AJC*. To further expose my business, I created Living Social and Groupon promotions to feature my in-home design consultation services at a discounted rate. Although these consultations were not very profitable, they were invaluable in marketing my business to an unknown and varied demographic.

An important tidbit to remember is that you must know your target market. Everything doesn't appeal to every consumer, but you must tap into what "your market" wants from you and give them that product and/or service at a fair price.

As I continued to build my brand, I recall a videographer coming to my home to shoot an Elevator Pitch video for *Black Enterprise Magazine*. The videographer was so impressed with my home furnishings and décor that he inquired about using my home as the set design for a show he was producing for the AIB Cable Network. While this show was airing, I was also able to secure a television commercial, which gave me further marketing reach.

As my decorating niche continued to evolve, I began searching online resources such as Craigslist and OfferUp to source furniture. I found folks selling high-end furnishings for pennies on the dollar; I was assured that most of these sellers had no idea the value of the pieces they were selling. I found pieces for my own home, but I didn't need *all* of the great things I found, so I began sourcing inventory for upcoming design projects. I decided to invest $2,000 from a tax refund and started buying furnishings and accessories to build my inventory. I would resell those items for a *significant* profit, and now I've built a 6-figure furnishings and accessories inventory from other folks' junk. This business became lucrative in a way that I never imagined possible. This *selling* business also became a third source of income for me that afforded me lavish vacations, home renovations, etc.

Since my home is located on a highly traveled street in my neighborhood, I was able to host garage sales to sell these furnishings and accessories. This idea worked for a period of time because I had minimal overhead, and I didn't have to advertise; My garage was staged like a furniture showroom so my customers had access to showroom quality pieces without showroom prices. The homeowner's association allowed me to have garage sales once a month, but after about three years, I had to upgrade my sales strategy. Traffic during the garage sales was a nightmare. I had to hire Atlanta police to direct traffic, parking was limited, and not to mention some of my neighbors became agitated about the increased traffic flow. These garage sales were extremely profitable, but I had to expand to a commercial location.

I knew I needed to expand but wasn't sure how I could afford a commercial location because a commercial location would dip into my profit margins, but in order *to make money, you have to invest money.* My other challenge was that I worked a full-time job, and I didn't trust anyone to run my operation when I wasn't there. How could a retail location operate without me being there? My realtor found a 1,000sf space for me in a commercial office park; it wasn't a retail location, so I didn't have to maintain normal retail hours. My store is named Savvy Home Boutique, and I'm open by appointment during the week and on Saturdays from 10 a.m. to 6 p.m. It's exclusive and quaint and close enough to my home and job that I can meet patrons quickly. Eventually, I may move to a larger retail location, but this exclusive locale is perfect for my business at this time.

I must mention that social media was important in building my brand. In essence, social media is free advertising that exposes you to an international demographic of consumers. I became a member of a thrifting group on Facebook where I would post my home décor and furnishing finds. My goal in posting was to educate folks that your home could look high end without spending tens of thousands of dollars on furnishings. Eventually, I started my own Facebook group Cents Savvy Home Décor which was a group dedicated to thrifting home décor furnishings and accessories. Within four years, that group had grown to over 39K members (which also grew by word-of-mouth referrals because the group is private). Like I've said before, your gift will make room for you, so through this group, I had a platform by which I could provide decorating tips, educate folks on how to integrate pre-owned furnishings into their décor, and market the furniture I was selling.

In closing, I knew I liked decorating, but no one had ever pushed me into exploring this as a career option. I doubted my skills because I never had any formal training in design. Everything I know about decorating and design and the business side has been learned by trial and error. I didn't have any design mentors to show me the way or to advise how I should charge for services. I have forged my own way through building my design business and opening my furniture store. I thank God for placing Gary in my life because he was the catalyst that facilitated this journey, and although we are no longer together as lovers, we will ALWAYS be the best of friends because he saw my gift BEFORE the world would ever experience it.

Knetta Lilly is CEO and principal designer for K Lilly Interiors (an interior design firm) and owner/proprietor for Savvy Home Boutique (a home décor and furnishings boutique) in Atlanta, GA. Knetta has been an interior decorator for 17 years, and she specializes in creating unique residential and commercial spaces with thrifted and second-hand furnishings and accessories.

Knetta received her B.S. in speech communication/public relations from Lamar University in 1991. Knetta has worked in the banking industry for 22 years and is currently employed at SunTrust Bank as a risk analyst. Her passion is interior decorating, so she operates two design-oriented businesses while working in banking full time.

Knetta's work has been featured in the *AJC* and on the AIB Cable Network. She also recently completed design work for a member of the R&B girl group, SWV.

Knetta is originally from Houston, TX, but currently resides in Atlanta, GA. She is single.

You can learn more about Knetta and her work through her website www.klillyinteriors.com and the following social media outlets:

- **Facebook**: https://www.facebook.com/KLillyInteriors/ and https://www.facebook.com/SavvyHomeBoutique/
- **Instagram**: https://www.instagram.com/klillyinteriors/ and https://www.instagram.com/savvyhomeboutique/

The Power of Networking and Collaborating

Ashley Little

Throughout my journey in corporate America and in entrepreneurship, relationships have been key for me getting to the next level. A true successful leader is one who reaches back and pulls forward. The key is believing in yourself and your vision. Successful businesswomen do not follow the crowd; we are willing to step outside the box. You have to be willing to take calculated risks and go after what you want in life no matter what.

I remember when I wrote my first book *Dear Fear Volume 2, 18 Powerful Lessons Of Living Your Best Life Outside Of Fear Collaboration Book*. This was the first time I was vulnerable with the world about different obstacles/challenges I have faced on my journey. I have always been a risk taker and was willing to jump no matter how I landed. We have to be willing to go the extra mile and ignore the chatter and distractions along the way. People are going to talk about you regardless, and if you can't handle being talked about, then success is not for you. When I first shared some of my obstacles/challenges, it was a relief because I was able to share my story in order to help someone else. My chapter was "Dear Fear You Can't Have My Power." I chose this title because there were many tests and people who attempted to make me feel powerless because of their insecurities. I have experienced times in my career in corporate America where I experienced seasons of discrimination and bullying. I refused to remain silent and always worked ten times harder to silence the noise. I have always been determined to stand up for myself and go around anything or anybody that tries to stand in my way. I have built my career in corporate America in different executive level positions, and I am continuing to build multiple successful platforms and businesses as an entrepreneur.

In order to be a successful business woman, one needs to have strategies to help her develop her skills and create and build successful networking and collaboration opportunities. Our destiny is tied to our connections, and you never know who will hold the key to your next opportunity. It is important for both people in every relationship to always bring value to the table and make room for others.

Some key strategies a successful businesswoman use are:

1. Believe in yourself- The fundamental key to success in business is self, and women are naturally known for underestimating their abilities.

2. Have a strong mission- Know your "why" and be willing to do whatever it takes as long as it is ethical.
3. Prepare your mindset- Success in business is highly dependent on mindset.
4. Be willing to fail- It is part of the process, and it is critical for every leader to embrace it. Everything in life is a lesson and is part of getting to the next level.
5. Increase your business skills- Always remain a student and be willing to invest in yourself and study your craft.
6. Make excellence a goal in everything that you do- Becoming a successful businesswoman requires thinking and acting strategically. It's a marathon, not a sprint.
7. Play the odds- You will succeed as long as you keep trying. Keep your eye on the prize and never give up.
8. Always look at the big picture- Keep your long-term goals in mind and always have a strategic plan to execute strategically.
9. Embrace your dreams- Surround yourself with your own vision and dream your own dreams.
10. Always find the lesson- Learn from every experience and circumstance whether good or bad. Roadblocks are only stepping stones to greatness. Allow yourself to be taught by every person you encounter. Most of all, listen more than you speak.

While working to develop yourself as a strong businesswoman, you also need to create and develop genuine relationships and to effectively collaborate with others. When you are networking and building collaborations, there are a couple of strategies you should be willing to do:

1. Be willing to serve- You should always have a servant leadership mindset.
2. Build value- We should bring value to everyone we meet. When we are networking and collaborating with people, we should come prepared with how we can help them get to the next level.
3. Developing reciprocal relationships- Every relationship you encounter should be reciprocal. Both people should be walking away with abundance.
4. Show up- Those who show up go up. Showing Up is critical to your success in corporate America and in entrepreneurship. No one is going to give you anything in life; you have to do the work and go get it.
5. Interview people- Your destiny is tied to your connections. Don't be afraid to support other people, and do not be intimidated by their success. It's not going to take anything away from you We Can ALL Win. When you interview people you want to connect with, you are taking the first step to building the relationship.

Lastly, continue to study and advance your work skills, even after you have achieved the position you desire. Half of the work of success is getting where you want to be; the other half is staying there. Share your victories and don't forget to celebrate and clap for yourself no matter who else claps. Building a successful business or becoming a successful businesswoman doesn't happen overnight; everything has a process. Staying humble, cultivating relationships, and staying grounded are key to getting to the next level.

Ashley Little is the founder/owner of Ashley Little Enterprises, LLC. She is your Media Maven specializing in media (Publishing, Radio/TV, Speaking, Public Relations, and Writing). Ashley believes in the currency of connections and encourages all of us to use our voices to create the world that we wish to see.

Ms. Little can be found online via Facebook (handle: Ashley Little) and Instagram (handle: _ashleyalittle).

Divine Wisdom for Successful Business

Dr. Valeka Moore

And there it is again, I thought. The W word again. How incredibly amazing and funny at the same time was it that I was being presented with an opportunity to contribute to a book about it. At that very moment, if never before, I knew that God was trying to tell me something. I mean, it was popping up everywhere. I could not get away from it. He was immersing it in every aspect of my life. Business, church, relationships, health, and most of all, my relationship with Him. Oh! Did I mention yet that the W word is *wisdom*?

We have all heard the word and know that it is an attribute that we should seek to have. Honestly, I thought I was doing pretty good in the wisdom department. But who knows? It's one of those things that you can never have enough or too much of. And clearly my Heavenly Father thought that I needed more.

It all started in early October 2018 when He dropped it in my spirit to complete a thirty-one day study of wisdom in the biblical book of Proverbs.

Honestly, I was all for it. For the past few months, I had been getting so many ideas for business. I had been writing them down for months as the ideas and visions moved from being fuzzy and unclear to seeming to come together quite nicely. I was excited as I felt that I had a pretty good blueprint and was close to execution. But God stopped me right there in my tracks. Before I moved forward with anything and shared any of the precious jewels that had been impressed upon my heart, I first had to complete this first step. Seek wisdom. Not only natural wisdom. But most importantly, the wisdom of God.

I was now experiencing a time that was reminiscent of when I first started out in business. I was a young business owner who had been called to be a business owner since childhood. I remember being 8 years old and drawing and coloring pictures to sell for 5 or 10 cents—25 if it was really good. Then moving to starting my own baby sitters club with a group of friends when I was eleven. Then moving to styling hair in my parents' living room, at church, or anywhere someone was willing to pay me for my services. When I went away to college, I remember saying I would become a psychologist and own a therapy practice. Fifteen years later, it was all coming full circle. The process to owning my therapy practice had begun. I was so excited and had so many ideas! I also wanted to do things right. I wanted guidance. I knew I was in a whole different world from being that little girl who explored and experimented within the entrepreneurial realm. This was for real!

I sought advice and mentorship from some of the most successful (in my eyes) business men and women whom I had access to. However, I remember moments in which my attempts to gather entrepreneurial insight left me feeling frustrated, rejected, abandoned, and even angry when my pleas for assistance were ignored or avoided, and promises to support were broken.

How could they do that to me? Why offer help if they weren't going to be true to their word? I held people hostage in my mind for displaying self-centered intentions or not holding up to their end of the bargain. But thankfully, I didn't allow that to stop me. I had to keep going. And in order to keep going and be effective in my entrepreneurial quest, I had to work through the hurt, frustration, and any notion that these individuals had an obligation to help me start my business. I was reminded that the word of God states that all things work together for the good of those who love the Lord and are called according to His purpose (Romans 8:28). Although I experienced some anxiety, which was natural for anyone stepping out of their comfort zone and pursuing something new, I knew deep down in my spirit that I had been called to start my very own business. When I allowed myself to take my eyes off of the people and place them on God, I was able to see why things didn't work out the way I wanted in this situation and many other times in my professional journey.

Number one, if certain things had happened the way that I wanted or thought they should have, I would have gotten stuck. I would have become too comfortable, and complacency would have taken over and caused interference with the timing that God had purposed for what I was destined to do. The things that

I didn't understand before were all supposed to unfold just as they did to get me to that very moment in 2014.

Number two, if things had worked out the way that I thought they should have, it would have taken away from the glory that was totally God's, and it would have been instead given to man. And of course God is not going to allow that to happen. And I am grateful that He got me in check real fast. Even though it did not feel good then, I am grateful for how God worked everything out. And you can believe with confidence that when God gives you a word or makes you a promise, He is going to come through. And He surely came all the way through, beyond what I could have ever thought or imagined. When I stepped out in faith, He equipped me with what I needed, and He has continued to provide every step of the way.

I feel that I have been blessed with wisdom and sound judgment to make some good decisions and do a lot of things right in business. I have also been blessed to do some things wrong. You may have just taken a moment to backtrack to the previous sentence to see if I really said what you thought you read. Yes, I did say blessed to do some things wrong. You see, those are called lessons, and when we adjust our mindsets, we can acknowledge lessons as blessings. Lessons prepare us for what may be ahead and enable us to proceed with caution.

So months ago, as I began to enter into a new season of business, I thoroughly understood the importance of seeking wisdom. When I was leaving my last job to begin my business, one of my co-workers shared a scripture with me that has greatly impacted the way I operate in life and business and has also become one of my personal favorites.

"Seek ye first the kingdom of God and his righteousness and all these things shall be added unto you" (Matthew 6:33 KJV).

Now, I must admit that there have been times when I have gotten a bit off course with this principle; however, I never stray too far before I am reminded that I need to get back on track. That is why it was nothing strange when it was dropped in my spirit to study the book of Proverbs before moving forward. What I currently knew was good, but I needed more to sustain me in my next season. In this new season, it wasn't about doing business as usual or simply about me as an entrepreneur. It was about the assignment. The God-given assignment. It was the absolute realization that other than my obedience to God to be used as a vessel, my entrepreneurial calling had very little to do with me and how I wanted to do things and was much about the purpose that God had for me. I always say there is very little that we need to figure out because we have the one who knows all. God tells us in His word that he knows every plan for our lives (Jeremiah 29:11)! He is the giver of wisdom. So for me, it is a no-brainer. When I seek wisdom from Him FIRST, it helps me make wise business decisions. It helps me make wise personal decisions. I become positioned for the best professional and personal opportunities. I am led to work with the right coaches with the wisdom and knowledge that I need to keep moving forward in my entrepreneurial journey. And I am equipped with more wisdom to pour into someone else.

So, remember, my beautiful sister, wherever you are currently in your entrepreneurial or life journey, God wants to take you higher. The vision is still unfolding. He has so much more for you! Believe it! But we are limited without His wisdom.

If you seek Him, He is going to give you wisdom, and you will be able to operate in and exude the brilliance that could only come from the Father. And trust me, you're going to shine really bright!

Blessings, my sister! <3

Dr. Valeka Moore is a wife and mother. She is the CEO/founder of Brilliant One Unlimited, LLC and Empowerment Thru Expression, LLC Therapy Center & Mind Spa. She is also a licensed therapist and coach to leaders and visionaries. Affectionately known as Dr. V. and the Transformation Activator, she is passionate about empowering individuals to shift from being stuck, confused, and frustrated by teaching them strategies to transform their minds, businesses, and lives as they fully embrace and activate the next level of their God given purpose and brilliance!

Learn more about Dr. V from her website:
www.drvalekamoore.

From Selling Snow Cones in the Hood to Providing Psychiatric Care

Regina Nelson

I wrote this chapter with the hope of the readers understanding that all things work together for the good to them that love God and are called according to his purpose. It doesn't matter where your life starts, who your mother is, who your father is, or where you grew up. Your passion will push you past every hurdle to be the entrepreneurs you were created to be. My story is a lot like many others. I grew up on the south side of Chicago. My mother had seven children. I was the second child of seven, and I got my sister's hand-me-downs. My self-esteem was low because when I got my sister's clothes, they were too big. I was skinny as a teenager, so I would have to tuck in my clothes and pin them up to make them fit. Even as a child, I knew life is better than what I was living. How could I succeed? My mother didn't have an education neither did her mother. What would I do to make a living? The women in my family either were on welfare or depended on their husbands to provide for them. I became a teenage mother. The odds were against me. But I always knew in my spirit there was more for me. I knew life had more for me. I remember collecting pop bottles for cash. At that time, you could collect bottles and cash them in. Daily, I would make money. You see, determination is the driving force behind an entrepreneurial mindset. Everything around me spoke poverty. I started journaling, and it became a powerful tool and my get-away. I would write about the life I wanted to live. Taking care of my family and living in a big beautiful home. How you see yourself is key.

My life took a detour after I started dating one of the biggest drug dealers on the Southside of Chicago. I got pregnant with my second child. He became abusive, and I start self-medicating with cocaine because of my depression. I would snort cocaine from the time I woke up to the time I went to sleep. He started using his product so bad that he became paranoid. Alarm systems in the home, I couldn't leave the home without him letting me out. I became more and more depressed about the situation I was in. This lasted for nine years. Little did I know that what I was going through would be the very thing God would use to help others. "And we know that all things work together for good to them that love God to them who are the called according to his purpose" (Romans 8:28, KJV).

When I was able to leave that situation, I started selling snow cones and candy while going to school for nursing. Selling snow cones gave me a sense of service. People would buy snow cones and candy and talk about their problems. I became an instant therapist. I always had an answer for their problems. Eventually, people came for the conversation and spent money just so we could talk. During that time, I made a lot of money selling snow cones. When the season for snow cones ended, I met a psychiatrist and started a cleaning business in the Hyde Park area of Chicago. We would talk about her business helping people figure out their problems. She was passionate about her work. Everyone has the right to be passionate about what they do for a living. Everyone deserves to wake up excited about their lives. I was passionate about having a better life, so I attended college and obtain my GED, RN nursing degree and master's degree as a family nurse practitioner. Two successful small businesses gave me the self-motivation to persevere. "Do not despise these small beginnings" (Zechariah 4:10, NLT).

Later, I started working for a company as a psychiatric nurse practitioner. Three months later, I received an email for a mandatory meeting. During the meeting, management disclosed the company was going out of business in thirty days. From that meeting, I was not only passionate but determined to start my own business. Preparation met with opportunity that day. You must prepare for success. Success doesn't happen automatically. You have to be an active participant. If I wasn't prepared, the opportunity wouldn't have presented itself. I launched Optimal Neuroscience Services LLC. on September 1, 2018. I specialized in the prevention, diagnosis, and treatment of mental disorders including but not limited to psychological and interpersonal problems with individuals and families, and intervention for coping with stress, crises, and other problems. Can you see the hand of God in my life? I was determined and passionate about my pursuit of entrepreneurship. What I learned from the path my life took was I was destined to become an entrepreneur. Every experience prepared me to launch my business. "From selling Snow cones in the hood to providing psychiatric care."

"Your passion will push you past every hurdle to be the entrepreneurs you were created to be."

What is the driving force behind what gets you up every morning? Keeps you up late at night? Your passion is the driving force that brings great success. It pushes you past every hurdle you may face when starting a business. It is more than what you are going to get as an individual; it serves a greater purpose. It is important to understand that passion alone won't give success. Draw up business plans with short- and long-term goals. Look at where you realistically expect your business to be in three to five years into the future. Determination and a lot of hard work are needed to succeed.

"Self-motivation is the confidence that you believe you can conquer the world even if no one else think you can."

Entrepreneurs must be self-motivated and have the ability to push themselves past where they are currently are. The only limitations in our lives are the ones we put on ourselves. Looking to external factors and friends for motivation is fine; however, at the end of the day, you're the one who must put in the work. If you need to look outside your circle for motivation, watch a movie that you found inspiring, a TED talk, or an inspirational podcast. Writing down and setting goals is a way to keep focused and track progress, and doing so will encourage and motivate you.

"Taking Risks is the path to entrepreneurship, you will win some and you will lose some, both are equally important."

Successful entrepreneurs are accustomed to taking risks and understanding what risks should be taken. Average people play it safe and almost never become business owners. I risked it all, quitting a job with dependable income. I had to trust God for my business. You need a support system. My husband was supportive. I made mistakes along the way trusting people I should have never trusted. Business owners know the importance of taking some risks; win some and you will lose some, both are equally important.

"Give your business time to grow. Stay the course."

When times get tough, the best advice is what got you started in the first place. Remember Your Passion. Growing a business takes time and patience. When I started my business, there was a season where I didn't make any money. You can't give up, you have to stay the course. I had to learn how to survive after stepping out on faith. By cooking your meals instead of going out. Bring your lunch to work. You learn to be frugal with your finances. I knew it was only temporary, I learned patience. The Bible states, "Let perseverance finish its work so that you may be mature and complete, not lacking anything" (James 1:4, NIV). Our true path for our lives cannot be figured out. God has a plan already prepared for us. Our job is simply to listen, and in the listening, drown out the noise of doubt. We will be given the guidance we need to do the work. Had I listened to those voices that told me I would be a single mother on welfare for the rest of my life, I would have never taken a step forward. "No one in your family had a business." Those voices were negative, but I stayed the course because there was always a voice that spoke louder about my future.

"You deserve a standing ovation. Now enjoy the fruits of your labor."

All the hard work and sacrifices have paid off. I've always had confidence in what my business could do. Prayer does change things. When you're in the business of serving others, you will succeed. Statistics report that more than 80 percent of new businesses that fail do so because they don't have enough money coming in to pay their bills. Statistics predict that you should prepare to run three years before you make money. My business did very well in the first year.

Regina Allen is a native of Chicago, Illinois, and currently lives in Indiana. Regina is a wife and mother and CEO/founder of Optimal Neuroscience Services LLC. She is a health coach, mentor, minister, author, family nurse practitioner (APRN), MSN, FNP-C, and she has served on the board of "Brother's Keepers" and Society of Nurses in Advanced Practice (SNAP). She has worked in various healthcare capacities as a psychiatric nurse practitioner. Additionally, Regina is passionate about serving her community within and outside of her local church. She is a co-author in two books, *I'm a Praying Wife* and *What Is a Courageous Woman*, and she has served as one of the lead roles in the stage play, *With God I Can Win*. Regina expresses her strength of the human spirit in the way she serves others.

Learn more about Regina by visiting her on:

- **Facebook**: (handle: regina.allen)
- **Instagram**: (handle: reginanelson)
- **LinkedIn**: (handle: regina.nelson.allen).

The Making of an Entrepreneur: From LA to LLC

Dr. Lisa Cox Romain

"The size of your dreams must always exceed your current capacity to achieve them! If your dreams do not scare you, they are not big enough." -Ellen Johnson Sirleaf

I was born and raised in Los Angeles (LA), California, the land of opportunities, glitz, and glamour. When I was a little girl, I got my first taste of the "good life." My kindergarten teacher had no children, and I was her favorite student. She lived in Bel Air and drove a 911 Porsche. She would often take me home with her and treated me as if I were her own daughter. After many rides in the Porsche and trips to her beautiful Bel Air estate, I thought, *This is the good life, and I want it.* Even as a little girl, I knew I had to work hard to acquire the lifestyle that I had become accustomed to and that no one would hand it to me on a silver platter. I don't have a beautiful home in Bel Air or drive a 911 Porsche; however; my life experiences in kindergarten and other pivotal moments in my lifetime sparked my passion for entrepreneurialism. I've always wanted to be my own boss, come and go as I please, run things with excellence and integrity, have various streams of revenue and income, help people, and enjoy life. I wanted a career where I worked smarter, not harder. I didn't want it to seem like work at all. I believe that if you do what you love, the money will follow. You will gravitate to those opportunities and network with people who can expose you to treasures associated with your passion, and you will want to be in the room where conversations are taking place about your passion.

As life would have it, I followed in the footsteps of my kindergarten teacher and became an educator. Although contributing to the lives of little people's minds was not my passion as she had done for me, I decided the way I wanted to help people was to identify my ideal population. I wanted to work with adults. I became a college professor, counselor, organizational psychologist, and licensed clinician. As a higher education professional, students would come to me, pouring their hearts out over issues that were traumatic and life changing. I thought, *Do I have a sign on my office door that says, if you are hurting, come on in?* or *If you are having problems with alcohol, substance use, or an abusive relationship, come on in?* These experiences did not seem to make sense at first until I reflected on other childhood experiences. As a little girl, I would often stare out of my living room window to look at the action in the neighborhood. I would see a man who was so handsome. He looked like Billie D. Williams, the kind of man I wanted to be my husband. This man was so fine. I would see him with a woman, they would be smiling, holding hands, and I thought, *What a man.* One day, as I was looking out of the window, I saw this same couple in the street fighting each other. The woman was on the ground screaming, and the man was beating her like a boxing ring opponent. No one stopped him. I was in shock, traumatized. People were outside looking at this fight, and no one helped the woman. Not long after the incident, I saw the same couple walking down the street, smiling and holding hands. I was so confused and thought, *I have to protect myself. If I get hurt, no one will help me.* From that moment on, I vowed to work hard, pursue formal education, and help other people. I did not know that in order to "help people" as a psychotherapist, I would have to take four licensing exams. I had been a college counselor, professor, and an organizational psychologist for over 23 years, and thought, *I got this.* Reality set in when I failed the licensing exams a total of four times. Although the failures were devastating, I did not give up and finally became a licensed marriage and family therapist and licensed professional clinical counselor.

What I learned most from life experiences is that my passion for wanting to become an entrepreneur came from "joy" and "pain." I wanted to create something, sustain momentum to build it, leave a legacy, and not give up when things got hard. These experiences defined my purpose and sparked a passion to help empower people to succeed. Passion motivated me to become an entrepreneur. In 2013, I took risks without knowing if my business ideas would succeed or fail, and launched a Limited Liability Company (LLC) and a Non-Profit (501c3), and a subsidiary company, Cox, Romain, Walker Divorce Mediation in 2016. Cox Romain Psychological Services, LLC is a counseling and consulting firm empowering organizations and individuals to develop and achieve goals that lead to success. The non-profit organization, New Beginnings and New Hope, serves the needs of those who have been impacted by domestic violence, sexual assault, substance use, and the criminal justice system. However, none of these business endeavors would have been possible if I did not consider my life experiences and wrote down the vision God had given to me. I couldn't just "think about it," "dream about it," or "talk about it." I had to "be about it." I had to "Write the vision, and make it plain" (Habakkuk 2:2 KJV). I had to make the vision a reality. I wrote down date-specific business goals, identified objectives, created a strategic plan and evaluation process, and assessed resource allocation. I had to decide if entrepreneurialism was attainable or if it needed to be put off to a later date. I trusted the process and relied on Proverbs 3:5 NIV, "Trust in the Lord with all your heart and lean not on your own understanding" as my "faith walk" scripture. I had to take care of myself, embrace life, and see the vision to completion.

Someone is waiting on your talents and skills to solve their problems. Passion, purpose, and pain will take you places you don't want to go, allow you to take risks when resources are not plentiful, and cause you to stay committed even when you want to give up. You are a multifaceted individual, and no one can do the same thing that you do in the way that you do it. A few things that helped me confidently launch my business endeavors were to assess my interests, values, skills, and personality. Consider the following strategies of success in becoming an entrepreneur.

"When you do what you love and what you're purposed to do, success will follow."

Identify Your Passion. Think about what you would you do if you weren't paid for it. Consider what keeps you up at night, is constantly on your mind, what gets you mad, and what you are willing to protect. You are the solution to a problem. Purpose comes from life experiences, which leads to passion.

Get to Know "You." Take career assessments that will help you identify your values, interests, skills, and personality. Evaluate your failures and successes, and pay attention to what people say you are good at doing. Don't be a counterfeit. Don't let people brainwash you into thinking that you are only capable of doing what they believe you should do. Don't let people strip you of your passion and God-given talents. Give yourself permission to explore "Why" you exist, "What" legacy you want to leave on this earth, and "How" you are going to pursue your life purpose, despite the odds. You are your best investment; no one can do you better than "You."

Stay Focused. You have two eyes, two ears, and one mouth. Be wise and listen to the Holy Spirit's guiding. Stop the negative "self-talk." Quit telling yourself you are not cut out to be a "Boss Lady," a businesswoman. Your eyes and ears are in front of you for a reason, to keep pressing forward. God did not put eyes in the back of your head to keep looking in the past, dwelling on business failures of investing money that did not produce a monetary profit, or wondering why He allowed a business to launch when you are not sure how things are going to be paid. When you keep turning around to look back at what is not working, it makes it hard to stay focused, and you might feel like giving up. Surround yourself with people who can encourage and motivate you to take risks for what you believe in. Each step is an investment toward a bigger goal. Stay focused and don't get off track.

Be Committed. Research the latest trends in your passion and get educated. Stay committed to your business endeavors even when it gets hard and you feel like giving up. Your industry decides what education and experience is needed for your entrepreneurial business. Not everyone needs a college degree; however, education leads to more opportunities. Stay committed to the business journey, and enjoy the fruits of your labor. I love to help people realize their potential and pursue their passion. I provide counseling and clinical services as often as I can, whether professionally or just by an encouraging word. Create a social media presence. Develop a website; join professional associations; create a LinkedIn account; do a podcast; attend business workshops; send out emails, tweets (Twitter), or Instagram posts with a quote of encouragement or leadership strategy. Keep a journal and write down ideas that will build and keep the business ideas flourishing.

Identify Opportunities. Who is in your sphere of influence? What people, places, and things are "passion drainers"? Evaluate the "good" and "bad" people around you, and assess what type of influence they have in your life. Connect with people who can help you network with others in your career field or get you in a business meeting to hear information that would take your business to the next level. Identify opportunities, build your assets, work on strengthening your weaknesses, and be aware of threats to your business venture. Your mental and emotional well-being is the key to success. Eliminate people, places, and things that kill your entrepreneurial passion. You want to thrive, not just survive.

Take Care of Yourself. Spend time alone and get to know the authentic "you." Assess what you like and what you don't like. Set boundaries for what you will tolerate in your life and eliminate anything that is toxic. Anything that drains your passion and blocks your purpose is unhealthy. Treat yourself with healthy things that make you feel good. Peace is priceless. Pursue what brings you the most peace, and watch your entrepreneurial passion arise.

Embrace Distractions. Look at "problems" as "opportunities." "If there is no growth, there is no change." "If there is no change, there is no growth." Identify a problem, create a solution and you will never be broke a day in your life. When life happens, it can be a distraction, and people will need your services to help them find a solution to their problems. Be a problem solver.

As a little girl, I was exposed to the "good life." I slept in a Bel Air home and rode in a 911 Porsche. I also experienced failures and successes that were humbling and life changing. However, none of these experiences would have sparked my passion to become an entrepreneur had I not paid attention to my life purpose and the needs of others. I took my "joys" and "pains" and turned them into businesses that solve problems. Take time to explore your passion and understand your purpose. Find problems and create solutions. Your passion is the making of an entrepreneur.

Dr. Lisa Cox Romain is an organizational psychologist, licensed marriage and family therapist, licensed professional clinical counselor, and certified Department of Transportation Substance Abuse Professional. Dr. Lisa is the president and CEO of Cox Romain Psychological Services, LLC, a counseling and corporate consulting company, and she is also the founder and executive director of New Beginnings and New Hope, a non-profit organization serving those impacted by domestic violence, substance use, child abuse, and CRW Divorce Mediation. Dr. Lisa is a counselor and professor at Palomar College and a professor at the University of Phoenix. She is the California Association of Marriage and Family Therapists Board Secretary, California Association for Licensed Professional Clinical Counselors Inland Empire Regional Coordinator, and the Coalition Against Domestic Violence of Orange County Vice President. Dr. Lisa is a certified domestic violence counselor, facilitates 52 Week Batterers Intervention

Programs and Child Abusers Treatment programs, Domestic Violence, Anger Management, and Substance Abuse services.

Stuck in the Comfort Zone

La'Sha'Rae Spencer

We as people often paint this picture of a perfect world in our mind, and when things don't go according to our perfect plan, we give up. Understanding that life comes with ups and downs gives us the courage to push forward when bad times do happen. Growth comes with many adversities, and understanding that failures along the way is what truly makes us successful is important.

When things get hard, do you give up? Do you tell yourself you don't care because you're afraid if you try and fail you now have to walk around with failure on your chest? Failure is only the obstacle that points us in the right direction. Do you understand that fear of failure and rejection is the number one reason why people are stuck today? We all know that life can have many challenges, but we can't let those challenges stop us from finding our true purpose in life. We must persevere no matter what obstacle comes our way.

I personally truly have real love for all of my ex-boyfriends because of all the lessons I learned with each breakup prepared me to be a better wife for my husband. Today, I am proud to say I have been married for five wonderful years. If I looked at each breakup, five to be exact, as failures and got stuck in my head telling myself I'm not good enough, no man will ever love me, all men are dogs, and ultimately becoming a bitter and unhappy person because I told myself to; there is no way I could be the wife and mother I am today. I had to allow myself to truly let love into my life and enter each relationship differently without comparing it to the last.

What we think about ourselves sets us up for where we want to go in life. As a teenager, I played Remy Ma's song "Conceited" over and over again until I learned every word. For me, that song taught me how to love myself. Yes, I know the content isn't great, but it gave me so much confidence. It drove some of my family crazy. I sang it everywhere I went at the time. I did have many insecurities, but one thing I did know for sure was that I loved myself, and success wasn't an option. I was taught to love myself from my mother. When people called me conceited, she used to say, "Excuse me! Tell them what I told you," and I would immediately say, "I'm not conceited. I'm confident." I must have said this statement hundreds of times. She told me I could be whatever I wanted and not to let anyone stop me and never settle for less. Her words taught me to be confident in myself no matter the circumstance and never to give up on myself; failure wasn't an option. To this day, I hang on to my mother's every word. There are many things that I have learned over the last ten years, and having a positive attitude at all times is one of them. When doors close, a job rejects me, or things don't go my way, I don't get angry or upset. I stop and think what I could have done better, or I simply say it wasn't for me and move on. I know what you're thinking: yea, yea, this all sounds great, but life isn't a fairy tale. Remember, we are in the driver's seat to our destiny, and it's up to you to get to your perfect destination.

At the young age of 17, I left to start my journey as a freshman at Grambling State University. It wasn't until I went back home during winter break that I realized how many people were STUCK! I had been introduced to this whole new world that was rich of education, and for the first time, I was around people who truly supported me. Not only my classmates but my teachers also believed in me, and everyone around me wanted more out of life. My first winter break going home was different. I noticed that nothing had changed; everyone was doing the same thing they were doing when I left, smoking weed and stressing over how to pay bills, and this happened over and over again over a three-year span. I made the decision my junior year that I wasn't going home for summer breaks. Three months was way too long, and holidays were enough. The idea that the people in the place that I called home weren't growing scared me, and to make matters worse, challenging someone's ideas wasn't ok, and I enjoyed the idea of challenging people's thoughts. It helped me better understand people and their thought process. I felt empty like I didn't belong in the place where I called home. I felt different my whole life, but this time was different. I felt sad for the people back home because they had no idea about life outside of Lynwood, Compton, and LA and that this world was full of opportunity and freedom to become the best version of themselves. Like most people, they were STUCK in the comfort zone.

S.T.U.C.K.

Safe

At times, we find ourselves afraid to take the next step in life because we fear the unknown. It's easy to stay in the environment in which we feel safe, and plus our family and friends are there. Think about it like this—you have been going to the same grocery store over the last 10 years, and you know where everything is, and one day you walk in and everything has been changed around, and I mean everything. Do you walk out the store? More than likely not. Most of us will use signs or ask someone who works in the store to help us find what we need. Although change may turn life as we know it upside down, remember to follow the signs and ask questions along the way. If the bumpy road ahead equals success, is it not a road worth taking? Safety makes us complacent and hinders our ability to grow, and growth leads to success.

Trapped

Who am I? is one of the most difficult questions to answer. Most begin by telling us about their career or what type of parent they are, but who you are at your core is what truly defines you. What are your likes and dislikes? What morals do you uphold? How do you see yourself? You have to build a strong sense of self-awareness. Take time and find yourself. Look for yourself if you feel like you're getting lost in the world that's wrapped all around us. Don't get trapped in your head believing negative thoughts you created. Speak life into yourself. Tell yourself "I'm good enough" every day. It starts with a thought, so we have to change our thought process by having a positive thinking pattern.

Under Educated

Learning new things prepares us for the success ahead. The world should be our classroom because there are many lessons to be learned. The world we live in is constantly changing, and new information is developing every day, but we limit ourselves when we are unwilling to learn new things. Finances, relationships, stress, depression, organization, or even parenting, no one is perfect. We all have things to learn, so read, research new information that's out in the world, get your friends and family involved in the new things you are exploring. Just learn no matter what, and don't be afraid to say you don't know, and ask questions even the stupid ones, and if you don't know what something means, look it up. Make Google your best friend.

Closed-minded

I'm so stuck in my own ways, no one can tell me what to do or how to do anything, and don't they dare try to tell me their point-of-view. Are you unable to see past your own set of values and refuse to see others' points of views, therefore unwilling to learn new ideas? This will have you STUCK right where you are.

Keeper

Sometimes, we find ourselves stuck in a mad place because we are taking care of everyone else. Early on, I believed that it was a bad thing that I was so selfish and that being self-centered was a bad look. Where I'm from, to be full of yourself was frowned upon. When you're on an airplane and have small children, the flight attendant says put on your oxygen mask first before putting on any small children. Can't help other people if you need help yourself. Take care of home first. Once you are solid on your two feet, now it is time to give back. We can't become the best version of ourselves with the weight of everyone else holding us back.

Changing your attitude toward life, you can find a positive in every situation, and I promise great things will begin to happen by changing our thought process. What we think about ourselves is the driving force to what we will become in life. The mind is so powerful. Believe in yourself and stop at nothing. Don't get stuck in a box you created for yourself. Your environment doesn't define you; you define your environment.

La'Sha'Rae Spencer was born and raised in Compton, CA, by way of Lynwood, CA. She and her husband of six years have two beautiful children. LaShaRae received her BA from Grambling State and later received a master's degree in psychology from The University of Phoenix. As a Navy wife, she knows first-hand what a struggle it is to move a family to a new place. She has helped many people learn how to successfully balance work, parenting, and a career. Her greatest fulfillment in her work is seeing people reach their full potential.

Learn more about La'Sha'Rae on Instagram (handle: Lifecoachrae) and her website: https://lifecoachsharae.com.

From Pain to Purpose: The Movie

Lindsey Vertner

FLASHBACK

I took a deep breath and hung up the phone, and tears started streaming down my face. I bawled at my desk for at least five minutes. I mean cry-me-a-river, ugly-snot-face crying!

Wait! You may be wondering, "What in the hell is she talking about?!" Well, it was the first of many meltdown moments in my entrepreneurial journey, and you've probably experienced a moment…or twenty… just like that! Let me back up, and tell you how this all began.

REWIND

In 2007, a "fatal" car wreck left me brain-dead and paralyzed. The car I was driving had done back flips off of the side of the highway before landing upside down in a ditch. After being cut out of the mangled car, I was pronounced brain-dead on the scene. I was flown by emergency helicopter to the nearest trauma hospital, where despite being pronounced brain dead a second time, surgeons attempted to relieve pressure from my brain and piece my skull back together. One blood transfusion and multiple surgeries later, doctors didn't expect me to make it through the night.

When I woke up in the hospital a week later, I had no clue where I was nor what had occurred over the previous days. I just knew I couldn't see, couldn't talk, couldn't move, and I was not at home. As my team of specialists filled me in on my countless injuries, I could blurrily see my mother sobbing near my bedside. I thought to myself, *Thank God I'm alive!*

FAST FORWARD

My physical recovery was nothing short of miraculous. I spent all day, every day—seven days a week—in various therapies: occupational therapy, physical therapy, shock therapy, cognitive therapy, you name it! I did it! My medical team was still shocked that I walked out of the hospital in exactly one month's time. For the record, it was a slow wobble with a cane, but I was up and moving, nonetheless. Although my body was healing swiftly on the outside, my inner healing took much longer. It was this emotional journey that opened the door toward walking in my purpose.

PUSH PAUSE

Doctors had prepared my family that I might not be the same person when I "come to." This ended up being a true and false statement at the same time. False – my personality remained the same. True – my focus, memory, and self-worth drastically changed. To this day, I suffer from mixed episodes of short- and long-term memory loss. I never know when I will remember or forget something. I could forget my thought mid-sentence. I could go downstairs to get a book, and by the time I got downstairs, I'd be in the kitchen getting a snack and back upstairs–book still on shelf.

Sometimes it took me hours to get focused on a task, and if that focus was broken in the slightest way…I'd have to start all over again. This was extremely frustrating for me because previously, things came to me easily and I caught on quickly. I started to have feelings of "why me?" and "what is my purpose in all of this?" I was already a perfectionist. So, the fact that I struggled to understand things caused me to be extremely critical of everything I did or said. Of course, I've since learned how to navigate these mental hiccups, but it takes regular maintenance and an increased self-awareness. It also didn't help that people were calling me "miracle woman." That is a lot of pressure to live up to, and I didn't feel worthy enough to hold that title. I had a fear that I would let everyone down. I feared letting myself down. I feared that…I wasn't…good enough!

SPEED IT UP

I started an intense self-improvement journey and realized that "I'm not good enough" was a subconscious limiting block that stemmed from my childhood experiences. So like many others, I set out to prove that I am in fact good enough. I did that by going back to school to get my master's in professional counseling because after all, my doctors said I wouldn't even be able to finish my bachelor's degree – let alone a master's! The joke was on me though because graduate school was the worst, but it also forced me to heal things that I didn't know needed healing.

During this time, I became a self-improvement junkie. Books, courses, events – if it was about personal development, I had it or did it! As I began coaching myself and those around me, I decided to focus my education around life coaching. I started to recognize that other women were struggling with the same belief of not feeling good enough, not feeling worthy, or allowing fear to dictate their actions. This is when hundreds of puzzle pieces started to fall into place, and my purpose became clear. The pain from my wreck had a purpose that was bigger than me. Despite having a successful business in direct sales, in 2015, I made the intentional shift to walk fully in my purpose!

PUSH PLAY

What is that purpose? I am an award-winning, personal development coach, transformational speaker, and Amazon #1 best-selling author. I teach ambitious, busy women around the world how to balance their lives by putting themselves first without guilt! I teach the developing, female entrepreneur how to identify her purpose, heal her limiting blocks, and create an action plan toward building her business. I speak life into audiences all over the world as a speaker. I'm the go-to expert for self-mastery. I teach others how to make shifts in the 3 pillars of self: self-care, self-worth, and self-discipline. It didn't come easy though!

Despite all of the work I've put in, as I mentioned previously, occasional meltdowns are par for the course. Everyone wants to highlight the glitz and glam of being an entrepreneur, but really…it's a constant roller coaster of highs and lows. I want to share three tips that seem so simple but are hard for many to implement.

TAKE "ACTION!"

SCENE ONE

You MUST make self-care a priority to survive as an entrepreneur. If you don't, you'll have MORE than your fair share of meltdowns and will not survive. Between being a wife, being a mother of two, being a graduate student, working an unpaid internship at the time, and fulfilling all of my other roles as a woman, I had a lot on my plate. I'm sure you can relate!

On this particular day, I had received bad news after bad news after bad effing news all within one hour. On my last call, I took a deep breath, hung up the phone, and the floodgates opened. I gave myself five minutes to feel all of those emotions before taking the rest of the day off. I went to sleep until it was time to pick up my children and slept like a baby. After I took time for myself, my mind became clear, and I could create solutions to the problems. However, creative problem solving cannot be done from emotional places. Whatever you must do to fill yourself up – DO IT! And do it regularly! Whether you need to take a nap, take the weekend off, get a massage, watch Netflix, have a drink with friends, whatever - you must prioritize self-care time.

Make a list of ten things that relax you and bring you peace and or joy. Spend time every day or at minimum, each week performing these things. You can't drive a car on an empty tank. Your mental and emotional state is the metaphorical car that drives everything you do! Fill 'er up!

SCENE TWO

Create boundaries for every relationship in your life. Family, friends, children, spouse, clients, co-workers, everyone! A lack of boundaries is reflective of our sense of self-worth. The lower your sense of self-worth, the lower amount of boundaries you have with others. In other words, *because I do not value my time, I allow my clients to contact me however they want, whenever they want. Because I do not value my well-being, I allow my friends to take advantage of me on a consistent basis.* Of course, these words aren't spoken directly, but actions speak louder than words. These are subconscious behaviors, which mean they sit below the conscious awareness, and you don't recognize what you're doing.

Schedule 30 minutes of uninterrupted time, and take some deep breaths. Take a moment to write down the most significant relationships from your past and present. Go through each relationship and identify the strong emotions that you feel. Reflect if the relationship evokes more negativity or positivity. Reflect how the memories indirectly shape your current beliefs and behaviors. How is this affecting your business? Create, adjust, and/or implement boundaries accordingly. (Note: You will likely need outside help to truly heal this area. However, awareness is your first step.)

SCENE THREE
Take accountability for your actions (or lack thereof). When things aren't going our way, it's easy to point the finger at others. However, true results occur when we are able to recognize how we are contributing to our struggle or success. EVERYTHING we do (or don't do) moves us forward, back, or keeps us in the same place. Remember that progress is better than perfection, and it is okay to make mistakes. What is important is that you keep moving forward. Being successful is a marathon, not a relay. Perform periodic self-evaluations in all aspects of your business and life. Be honest with yourself and adjust as needed, but don't forget to allow yourself grace!

ROLL CREDITS
You are the writer, the director, the producer, and the leading actress in the movie that is your life! You decide who your supporting characters are. You have the ability to rewrite any prequels that no longer serve you. You have the ability to create a sequel that you desire and make it your reality! You must push past the pain and keep going. I could've listened to the gloomy outlook doctors had for my life, but instead, I chose to take my life into my own hands. I chose to put in the work to achieve the life I deserved living. I chose to create a business that helps others to achieve the lives they are worthy of. Always remember that you are the star of your life and business!

If you need help on your personal or entrepreneurial journey, send an email to GetHappy@LindseyVertner.com to see how we can work together. Visit www.LindseyVertner.com for motivational content, event bookings, and to sign up for updates on my forthcoming anthology, *First Class Life: Transformational Lessons to Create a Life Full of Purpose, Fulfillment, & Happiness.* Follow me on Facebook, Instagram, YouTube, and all social media at @LindseyVertner. If you want to connect in person with myself and other likeminded women, sign up for event updates at www.TheUnleashedWoman.net.

A 2007 "fatal" car wreck left **Lindsey Vertner** brain dead and paralyzed. Using her unparalleled perspective as a coach and speaker, she pushes clients toward success in their personal and professional lives. Lindsey's expertise centers around overcoming obstacles, work-life balance, and the "3 Pillars of Self" (self-care, self-worth, and self-discipline and how each of these areas affect our lives subconsciously). Lindsey is co-founder of The Unleashed Woman – a nonprofit organization that uplifts women of all backgrounds through empowerment events. With a master's in professional counseling, Lindsey is a graduate of both Indiana and Liberty Universities. Connect with her at www.LindseyVertner.com.

Wisdom or Mistakes?

Stephanie Welch-Lewis

I'll take wisdom, and that will be my final answer.

Most people decided they wanted to become a business owner, but my journey started with if you don't open the door for me, damnit, I'll build my own house and add my own door!

I worked for a racist custom drapery company. I know people use this term loosely, but the owner explained to me that she grew up a racist. She hired me because I have a very light complexion for a black lady—her words to me, and she didn't think her clients would be offended with working with me. I needed this job and more work experience, so I accepted the position. I worked for this company approximately six months before I couldn't take it any longer because of many racist comments followed by the statement "but you are different."

During this time, my husband was recovering from a bone marrow transplant, and we traveled back and forth to Detroit for doctor appointments three times a week. This made working a traditional interior design job not an option for me. Life had given me lemons, and I didn't feel like making lemonade, so I made a lemon meringue pie instead. I started my company Beautiful Designs by Stephanie with no money and the faith the size of a mustard seed. I have made mistakes along the way, but I learned from them, and I would like to share some of my 20+ years of wisdom to help you if you decide to start a business. You will still make mistakes, but hopefully with a road map, you can avoid the bumps and potholes I've already hit.

My name is Stephanie Welch-Lewis, and I am the owner of Beautiful Designs by Stephanie. This is an interior design company that specializes in window treatments. When I was approached to become a part of this project to talk about wisdom, my first thought was wisdom should come from a seasoned person. I soon realized that the date on my birth certificate qualified me to be considered seasoned, and after operating my business for many years, I have definitely become wiser in business.

The best advice that I learned is it's better to be prepared and not have an opportunity than to have an opportunity and not be prepared. I have been on both ends of this quote. The experience that I remember the most is not being prepared. A friend of mine referred my business to her friend. When I arrived at the house, I couldn't believe this house, and the neighborhood was to die for. (Well, I wouldn't actually want to die, but you get the idea.) My specialty is in custom window treatments, but this client wanted more than custom draperies. My business cards listed a variety of services that I would provide. (Sidebar: I was trying to save money with the cost of my business cards, so I listed things that I would provide in the future.) The customer noticed all the services listed on my card and wanted some of the services that were on the card. The problem was I didn't have sources to carry these items at the time. This was my ideal customer, the one where you pray to God to send, but I wasn't prepared. Well, I blew that opportunity. I made a promise to myself I would never let this happen again! I would explain to the customer the services that I could complete or state I no longer offered services. Customers would appreciate the honesty, and you won't embarrass yourself and your company.

The next thing I would suggest is to give fair prices. This means fair to you and the customers. Many businesses are slow in the beginning, but not mine. I was swamped because my prices were too low, and the word must have spread. It seemed like everybody bought their blinds from me. I then noticed that I didn't make much money. I had no idea about profit margins or markups, overhead cost, or other business terms. I remember giving a customer a quote for custom drapery. I thought the quote was too expensive, so I gave her my best quote. I still thought the quote was too high, but that's the best I could do. I called the customer. I told her I had her quote ready.

"Let me sit down for this," she said.

"Yes," I said, "make sure you are sitting down." I explained to her that the size of her window is how we determined the cost. (I was working my way up to the price.)

When I told her the price, she gave a loud, "What!?"

"I know."

"Sears wanted twice that amount. When can you come get your money?"

The next day, I decided to check my competitors' prices and immediately raised my prices. Customers don't value your services if you are too cheap. This is especially true if they have received other estimates, and yours is much lower. They assume that your product will be inferior. My prices now are comparable but, in most cases, still lower. I now take into consideration all those business terms that I knew nothing about earlier in my business. When you know better, do better.

Another wisdom nugget is to offer great customer service by under promising, over delivering, effectively communicating, and showing appreciation. Custom draperies take approximately 6-8 weeks to complete, sometimes even longer. Just imagine if you purchased a big-ticket item and gave the person a deposit of half the amount, and you haven't heard from the company in 8-10 weeks. This is why communication is important. I inform my customers when the order comes in, when to expect installation, and follow up with thank you cards. One of the best investments for my business is note cards. I know you are thinking how in the world can that be the best investment for your business. I receive positive feedback constantly from my customers who thank me for sending them a thank you card. This is also an inexpensive way to stand out from your competitors.

Invest in yourself and your business. Make sure you stay current in your industry. You should attend conventions and classes, read books, or even watch YouTube videos to improve your knowledge of your products or services. Customers are very savvy now. I remember working with a client who wanted a particular style of chair that I had never heard of before, let alone knew how to spell. (That's why I'm not spelling it now). When I hung that phone up, I immediately researched the chairs and started calling companies to inquire about them. I'm laughing now thinking about how I was mispronouncing the chair name and the person on the phone kept correcting me. You should also invest in your brand. This includes a nicely designed business card, logo if necessary, professional headshot. What I'm about to say next I am still working on myself. You should always look neat and presentable at all times. You are a walking advertisement for your business.

I read a variety of books of successful people, and what most successful people have in common is they volunteer or work with a charity or cause. Volunteer at a local charity. This will give you an opportunity to meet people outside your normal circle and increase your networking circle. Develop a relationship with fellow volunteers before you go in for the kill… I mean pitch. Just wait until you hear these magic four or five magic words. SO, WHAT DO YOU DO? (Ding, ding, ding) It's showtime. Have a thirty-second commercial ready, and don't blow it. A thirty-second commercial is everything you want people to know about your business or services within 30 seconds. Don't use filler words, such as "um" and "like," and include a catchy tag line. A tag line is a phrase to make your business stand out. If you can't create an original tag line, then Google one. Next, exchange business cards so that you will have their information. They may not remember your name or your company name, but they may remember your tag line or service you provide. It's so funny that people who can't remember my name call me the Blinds Lady. I will take it because they know the services that I provide.

These are a few things to assist you with your journey in business. Sometimes, wisdom comes from being foolish. I have made some foolish, costly mistakes. One of my mom's favorite saying is "Bought sense is better than taught sense." I had no idea what in the heck that meant. I wasn't going to ask her because when she was quoting it, she was upset. Years later, she shortened it to "Well, I guess you bought that lesson." It finally clicked in what she was talking about. You can either let somebody tell you something, or you can learn it the hard way. My goal in sharing some tips is to keep you from buying the lessons.

Proverbs 4: 6-7 states, "6 Do not forsake wisdom, and she will protect you; love her, and she will watch over you. 7 The beginning of wisdom is this: Get wisdom. Though it cost all you have, get understanding."

Have a blessed journey.

Stephanie Welch-Lewis is the owner of Beautiful Designs by Stephanie. This is an interior design company that specializes in custom window treatments, bedding, upholstery, and accessories. Beautiful Designs by Stephanie has been in business for over 20 years. Stephanie's background includes an associate degree in interior design and being a window fashion certified professional and Hunter Douglas certified. Stephanie was also head designer at La-Z-Boy and a salesperson in the drapery department at a major department store.

Stephanie started this business with a dream, a sample book, and the faith the size of a mustard seed.

How This Women Changed The Landscape of Tax Business and Seeks To Help Others

Dr. Cozette M. White

Black women are the fastest growing demographic of entrepreneurs in the United States, according to *Fortune Magazine*. Margot Dorfman, CEO of the U.S. Women's Chamber of Commerce said, "We attribute the growth in women-owned firms to the lack of fair pay, fair promotion, and family-friendly policies found in corporate America."

Despite this statistic, many Black women, and women of color in general, are finding it increasingly challenging to traverse the entrepreneur landscape and secure venture capital funding. So one would ask, *"How do I create a business that is successful and profitable? More importantly, what is needed to sustain a business and expand?"*

Dr. Cozette M. White, managing partner for My Financial Home Enterprises, LLC, is an entrepreneur that has discovered how to grow and maintain a profitable business. White didn't come from an entrepreneurial background but learned lessons through her many wins and losses. White sat down with Next Generation Speakers (NGS) to discuss how she positioned herself to transition from welfare to winning by unlocking the code to her 6-figure tax business! She'll share what she's learned along the way and the business necessities every founder should consider.

CWM: What accounting and tax advice would you share with the readers?
Dr. White: Perhaps you are a first generation business owner...or simply so involved in the daily operations of your business that some key aspects of your business are overlooked and preventing you from elevating to the next level.

It's no question that being an entrepreneur is a journey that will help uncover your strengths, weaknesses, vulnerabilities, your resolve, and resilience. Most of us obtain college degrees, and we were unleashed unto the world and found ourselves in a corporate setting where all of the items I mention below are handled by specialized departments. Now that you have ventured out as a business owner, the learning curve may appear to be steep compared to your first couple of years on your first corporate job. Avoiding certain key mistakes can really help minimize some of the risks your business may face throughout various economic conditions.

CWM: What metrics have you incorporated into your business to achieve success?
Dr. White: I have a set of routine metrics that I live by each month in order to accomplish our goals. We track how many prospects with need to reach to obtain our annual goal and break that number down to how many per month, and number per day. We look at how many strategy sessions we need to conduct for the year broken down by month, by week, and by day. Our team meets two-three times per month to ensure we are tracking accordingly.

CMW: What other key components do you have to add in order to scale and grow?
Dr. White: We put our A-Team in place. This is pivotal to the business. As small business owners, we're concerned with meeting our payroll obligations when onboarding new employees. However, there are other options available to new business owners that are extremely cost-effective when building an A-Team. When onboarding, make sure you screen your candidates thoroughly before extending an offer to work with your organization.

Recordkeeping

Your business is growing in sales, and you know in order to meet demand and sustain the quality of your products and services, you will need a line of credit with the bank or an infusion of capital from investors. However, in an effort to save money starting out as a small business owner, you opted to maintain the books yourself. A few years have gone by, and you look up and realize you don't have a set of financial statements for each year you have been operating to show a loan officer this tremendous growth your business has experienced. The bank understands the numbers and what they will show to support your verbal claims and enthusiasm.

Not Utilizing Business Tax Deductions

One strategy for maintaining positive cash flow for your business is to maximize all applicable business deductions allowed by the IRS. The way to reduce your tax liability is ensuring you have adequate accounting records and documentation to report business expenditures that qualify as tax deductions on your tax return. Here are several to consider:

Advertising | Auto Expenses | Bad Debt | Hiring Your Children | Home Office Deductions | Legal & Professional | Meals, Travel & Entertainment | Start-Up or Expansion Cost | Self-Employment Retirement Plan

Not Seeking Professional Help

According to "Inc.," 48% of female business owners, almost half, cite a lack of available mentors or advisers as holding them back from growing their business. Don't try to be superwoman as you run a business, be a boss, a wife, and mother and still maintain your health and wellness throughout it all.

Having a team of legal and accounting professionals accessible to you is vital to the growth of your business. These professionals have years of experience and expertise and can efficiently and effectively handle the matters of your business. These service providers can partner with you and share the same goals of expanding your business.

Not Enough Insurance to Cover Business

Business insurance protects your investment by minimizing financial risks associated with unexpected events. Insurance coverage is available for every conceivable risk your business might face. Cost and amount of coverage of policies vary among insurers. You should discuss your specific business risks and the types of insurance available with your insurance agent or broker. Many entrepreneurs begin their small businesses in their homes.

Poor Cash Flow Management

Cash flow is the net change in your company's cash position from one period to the next. If you take in more cash than you send out, you have a positive cash flow. You have a negative cash flow if you have more cash outflow than inflow. Cash flow is a key indicator of financial health. A cash flow statement charts the flow of money into and out of your business. It's all about gauging liquidity — or cash on hand — so that you can make smart decisions about paying bills and buying additional assets or inventory.

Our Firm

We are a global financial consulting firm providing comprehensive accounting, tax, and business management services.

We are committed to helping **high net worth clients** and **healthcare providers** build successful enterprises. Our skilled team of financial experts have years of experience in providing exceptional service.

Our trained staff understands the unique challenges you face. As your trusted advisors, we work with you throughout the year to evaluate your business and ensure that your financial needs are met. Our critical analysis and practical solutions will identify business trends and opportunities for growth as well as help you improve the operations, efficiency and profitability of your business.

We are committed to helping our clients achieve and maintain financial freedom.

My Financial Home Enterprises has been featured in *Forbes Magazine* and named one of The Boss Network's top 50 companies two years in a row. As Cameka Smith, founder and CEO of the Boss Network put it, "*Without question she is brilliant at teaching others to leverage their unique gifts and qualities into a financial windfall.*"

Our Founder

Our founder, Dr. Cozette M. White is an acclaimed best-selling author, nationally recognized accounting and tax expert, international speaker, and philanthropist.

Dr. White is a resident Money Matter's Tax Expert for FOX40. Her excellent media credentials, professionalism, and outgoing personality have allowed her to provide expert advice on tax issues for CBS This Morning, NBC, ABC, and FOX television stations. She has been featured on numerous radio shows including Radio One and iHeart radio, and she's a recurring voice to millions, making regular appearances in various national media outlets, including *Black Enterprise*, *Forbes*, *Women of Wealth*, *Upscale*, *The Huffington Post*, and countless newspapers across the country. *Women of Wealth* dubbed White, "Wealth Builder Extraordinaire." Recently, Dr. White was awarded the President's Lifetime Achievement Award by President Barack Obama.

Dr. White is a giver! She is the founder and executive director of Achieving My Dreams Foundation, Inc. The organization grants scholarships to graduating high school seniors majoring in S.T.E.A.M. She is also involved in her community and is a member of Alpha Kappa Alpha Sorority, Inc.; the National Association of Black Accountants; and the National Black MBA Association.

A Note from Dr. White

I'd love to give you 45 minutes of my time for free where we can deep dive into your current business structure and tax strategy and see how you can take advantage of legal and ethical loopholes to save tens of thousands of dollars per year in taxes.

There's no obligation whatsoever. I won't hold anything back. I'll review your business entity structure, tax strategy, and accounting system to make sure you're maximizing profits and cash flow and minimizing taxes and waste. At the end of our call, you'll have a clear plan for what you need to do to boost your take-home pay by up to 50%.

If you want my help implementing the plan, then I'll be happy to talk with you about working together at the end of our call, but you absolutely don't have to become my client to get massive value out of our conversation...

Ready to Take Action? Let's Build Your Practice & Save You Tax!

If you want to take control of your financial future and keep more of your hard-earned money, book a free 45-minute strategy session with me here:
https://my.timetrade.com/book/K5XHS

I look forward to talking with you and helping you get clarity on how to create lasting wealth for you and your family.

Dr. Cozette M. White
Your Financial Physician

Business 101

How to Establish a Legal Business

1. File your DBA, LLC, S-Corp, C-Corp, 501C3 Status (with Article of Corporations and By Laws). I use incfile.com, and for everything, it's about $165 depending on your state. Note that as a DBA, you will never qualify for any business loan or credit. If you don't have the $165, you can still do business and get an EIN but get your LLC, S-Corp, C-Corp, 501C3 status as soon as possible. If you want to save $60, look up do-it-yourself Business Entity Filing. Make sure your business name doesn't have "real estate" or "investment" in it. Those Businesses Names are considered a Liability.
2. Get an EIN Number from the IRS; it's free. Apply at irs.gov.
3. Get a Duns Number from www.dandb.com; it's free. Your Dun Number is like your business Social Security Number.
4. Sign up for a Nav Account at nav.com; it's free. It's a free business credit monitoring company like Credit Karma but for your business credit scores.
5. Sign up on sam.org to do business contracting with the government free. Even if you don't want to contract with the government, signing up makes you a creditable businesses—and less likely to get audited.

6. If you have a home-based business, you HAVE to have a virtual business address. I use iPostal.com; the first payment was $65, and the monthly payments are $40 a month. This also includes a fax number, which you will need.
7. Fax Number and Business Phone Number: You can try myfax.com for $7.99 a month, but you should bundle with iPostal as it is cheaper. For the business number use Google Voice (free). To do so, make a Gmail account and sign up for Google Voice.
8. Business Email: Your email should be info@whateveryourwebsiteis.com–not Gmail or yahoo.com. I can sign you up for $13 a year with GoDaddy.
9. You must have a website: Even if it's a one-page site. I charge between $99-$2,500. Hosting is $9.99 a month for one site. You won't even get looked at without a website. You also need to set up social media business pages on Facebook, LinkedIn, Twitter, and Instagram. With that website, you will need a logo. A logo is like your business face, literally. Our cost is $80 for a custom logo, but get something. I can't stress having a logo enough. You will eventually need to get your logo trademarked. But you will not need it right away. You can wait a bit. Cost is $275 on ustrademarks.gov or incfile.com will do it for $575.
10. Business Validations – Submit your business listing for free on Google Business, Yelp, YP,

411(Note: There is a fee for 411, but I do not recommend paying it if your broke because eventually it will make its way there anyway for free.), List Yourself, and Super Pages. Also contact Verizon—you do not have to be a customer. Tell them you want to list your business in their Foreign Directory for $10. Do at least three of these!

11. Set up a business checking bank account with any local bank or credit union. You will need a copy of your DBA, LLC, S-Corp, C-Corp, 501 C3 Business Entity Status.
12. Trade Lines: These are lines of credit used to build up your business credit score given by Duns and Bradstreet. I use Uline and Quill. Let them know that you are a business and want to establish a Net 30 account. Order the products you need, and you have 30 days to pay on those products. After the full payment is made, the company reports your trade line to Dun and Bradstreet, and you will establish a business credit score. Scores are between 0-100. (Note: These companies will only report purchases over $50). Next, you will move from Net 30 Trade Lines to store business credit cards, such as Walmart, Best Buy, gas cards, etc. After that, business credit cards, such as Chase business, Visa, Mastercard, etc. Then, after 10 good tradelines on your report, you can get anything your heart desires like $50,000 to $500,000 business loans.

13. Business Insurance: Depending on the products you sell, some of you will need some business insurance and or business licensing with your state. For example, if your company works in/with food, realtors, medical needs, or construction, Incfile will have a search button in your account to see if you're State requires this for your business.

Now, you might ask, "Do I really need all this now?"

The answer is YES. If you're in business to make money, you need it all. If you don't have everything on this list, you will never get any type of business credit cards or loans, which you need to have capital for your business, or your business will drain you. Even if you do have excellent personal credit, banks and credit card companies will still want to verify that you're an actual business. Trust me—save yourself the heartache and do as much as you can on the list ASAP.

If you are approved for a business loan, you will need to provide the following information:

1. Business Name(s)
2. Business Entity (LLC, S-Corp, C-Corp, 501C3)
3. Business address, phone, fax
4. Business email
5. Website address
6. Duns number
7. EIN
8. Business checking/saving

9. Business' annual gross
10. Paydex Score (Duns and Bradstreet) (1-30, 40-70, 80-100) (*They Check for trade lines)
11. Credit Score (300–400, 500–600, 700-800) (*Won't matter if you have high business credit)

Aside from these things, loan companies will also want to know more personal information, such as if you rent or own your home or apartment, your address, phone number, etc. If you can't provide answers to the 11 things above, most places won't see you as a reliable, credited company.

So What If You're Broke?

If you can do all of the things on this list now, just spend the money and save yourself a headache. If not, you can still get your business up and running. Then take your profits to complete the list ASAP. The problem with this, however, is that you will have to edit every account you create with your new business information every time you're able to purchase something from the list. From your business entity, EIN, Nav, Duns number, website, bank accounts, and social pages, they all must have the same information on them.

The following suggestions are what you should be seeking to take care of—depending on your budget:

Broke Broke: *If you have very little to no money*

1. File your DBA, LLC, S-Corp, C-Corp, 501C3 Status -- $165
2. EIN Number -- Free
3. Business Address, Phone, Fax -- $65 / $40 monthly
4. Duns Number -- Free
5. Nav Account -- Free
6. Sam.org Account -- Free
7. Business Email/ Domain -- Name $25 a year
8. Submit Your Business Listing -- Free
9. Business Checking & Saving Bank -- $5.00
10. Setup Business Social Media Pages -- Free
11. Create Your Own Temporary Logo -- Free

Total: $260.00

Just Broke: *If you have a little money*

1. File your DBA, LLC, S-Corp, C-Corp, 501C3 Status -- $165
2. EIN Number -- Free
3. Business Address, Phone, Fax -- $65 / $40 monthly
4. Duns Number -- Free
5. Nav Account -- Free
6. Sam.org Account -- Free
7. Business Email/ Domain -- Name $25 a year
8. Submit Your Business Listing -- Free
9. Business Checking & Saving Bank -- $5.00

10. Setup Business Social Media Pages -- Free
11. Custom Logo -- $80
12. 1 Page Website -- $110, $10/month
13. Get Two Trade Lines -- $100

Total: $550

<u>In the Money</u>: *If you have the "bills" to pay the bills*

1. File your DBA, LLC, S-Corp, C-Corp, 501C3 Status -- $165
2. EIN Number -- Free
3. Business Address, Phone, Fax -- $65 / $40 monthly
4. Duns Number -- Free
5. Nav Account -- Free
6. Sam.org Account -- Free
7. Business Email/ Domain -- Name $25 a year
8. Submit Your Business Listing -- Free
9. Business Checking & Saving Bank -- $5.00
10. Setup Business Social Media Pages -- Free
11. Custom Logo -- $80
12. 5 Page Website -- $399, $10/month
13. Get Five Trade Lines -- $250
14. Trademark -- $275
15. Prices vary from $50 to $250

Total: $1,525

Made in the USA
Monee, IL
04 November 2026

67382848R00089